Counterpoint and Beyond

Counterpoint and Beyond

A Response to *Becoming a Nation of Readers*

Jane L. Davidson, Editor
Northern Illinois University

National Council of Teachers of English
1111 Kenyon Road, Urbana, Illinois 61801

Staff Editor: Timothy Tikhon Bryant

Book Design: Tom Kovacs for TGK Design

NCTE Stock Number 08768

Library of Congress Cataloging-in-Publication Data

   Counterpoint and beyond: a response to Becoming a nation of readers / Jane L. Davidson, editor.
      p.   cm.
   Bibliography: p.
   ISBN 0-8141-0876-8
   1. Reading (Elementary)—United States.   2. Literacy—United States.   I. Davidson, Jane L., 1934–
LB1573.C5577 1988
372.4—dc19   88-22541
                                                                        CIP

Contents

Foreword

When *Becoming a Nation of Readers** was published in 1985, the Commission on Reading of the National Council of Teachers of English was asked to comment on the suitability of NCTE distributing the volume. The range of opinion of the commission members concerning *BNR* was not wide. All members immediately expressed concern about the content of the report, and many feared that NCTE distribution would be tantamount to endorsement. Nevertheless, when a poll was taken, six of the twelve members voted to approve distribution on the grounds that NCTE must be a forum for a wide range of opinions and that we must not be in the position of being charged with suppression of influential information concerning literacy. The commission members' reservations concerning the report and the results of the poll were passed on to the NCTE Editorial Board, which voted to include *BNR* in the NCTE catalog.

The inception of the present volume took place at that time. Individuals on the Editorial Board as well as other NCTE members urged the Commission on Reading to respond vigorously to *BNR*. The commission's first responses came in the form of presentations at major conventions in 1986, including the NCTE Spring Conference in Phoenix, the International Reading Association Conference in Philadelphia, and the NCTE Annual Convention in San Antonio. During this time, members of the commission talked with language arts educators throughout the country and sensed their dismay and uneasiness concerning the influential report. Many of these teachers and researchers appeared on the Commission on Reading's programs, and many encouraged the commission to be about its business of presenting to the profession counterpoints to the positions presented in *BNR*.

Among those who nudged commission members was Jane Davidson. It soon became evident that the time to respond was *now* and that Jane was the one who could help us most expertly and efficiently with the task. Jane was commissioned to collect manuscripts and to

---

* Referred to throughout this volume as *BNR*.

edit the responses dealing with an issue that demanded clarification, candor, and civility.

Jane and the authors chosen have clearly accomplished the task given them, and have gone further: they have gone *beyond the counterpoint.* In the contributions to this volume readers will discover that the authors intrepidly but without rancor responded to *BNR* in two ways. When they saw shortcomings, they pointed out those failings. Then they either added breadth and clarity to the view presented in *BNR* or posited an alternative view that is supported both by research and practice.

The profession is healthier for the efforts of these authors and for the discussion this volume is certain to generate.

Dorothy J. Watson
Director, NCTE Commission on Reading

Introduction

Introductory statements in *Becoming a Nation of Readers** indicate that the purpose of the report was to summarize research findings and draw implications for instruction in order to provide for the improvement of literacy in our country. The report, widely distributed, has received national attention. Its recommendations are regarded by its authors as representing guidelines for instruction that they consider to be generally agreed upon by most reading authorities. A monograph entitled *What Works: Research about Teaching and Learning*, published by the U.S. Department of Education (1986), based part of its recommendations on information reported in *BNR*. This information was described by William Bennett, secretary of education, as "the best information available to the Department" (Bennett 1986, p. v). Many school districts throughout the country, pressured by their communities as well as state and federal agencies to improve literacy, are using the recommendations in *BNR* as absolute guidelines for change. While some of the concepts presented in *BNR* probably do represent agreement by reading authorities, numerous issues are discussed that would not be agreed upon by many reading authorities.

This monograph serves as a forum for the responses of a number of reading authorities to *Becoming a Nation of Readers*. Issues in *BNR* that are considered to be controversial, incomplete, or inconsistent are addressed; reactions and alternative recommendations for the improvement of literacy are set forth.

The opening chapter by Bloome et al. presents an analysis of the metaphors employed in *BNR* and raises serious questions about the appropriateness of those metaphors in describing research. Readers of *BNR* are warned to study carefully the impact and potential consequences of the metaphors when considering recommendations in the report.

Chapters 2 through 6 address issues related to beginning reading instruction. Davidson, Lia, and Troyer discuss the portions of *BNR* that concern emerging literacy and point out that child-centered,

---

* Referred to throughout this volume as *BNR*.

1

language-based programs for beginning reading instruction are more consistent with theory and research supporting emerging literacy than are formal instructional programs. Scott's paper also focuses on emerging literacy; however, she examines *BNR* to determine whether its recommendations can be applied to nonmainstream groups. The chapters by Hall, Holloway, and Bridge focus on word identification as described in *BNR*. Hall analyzes the recommendations concerning word analysis, particularly those concerning phonics instruction. She calls for educators to move beyond the debate about decoding and argues that educators who wish to follow the recommendations should do so from a whole language perspective. Holloway focuses on the difference between word-comprehension strategies and word-identification skills. She recommends that beginning reading instruction concentrate on meaning instead of sounds in order to acknowledge and provide support for the linguistic competencies of children. Bridge points out an inconsistency between the interactive, constructivist theory of reading presented in *BNR* and the instructional practices for phonics suggested. She presents alternative instructional practices that represent greater consistency with such a theory.

In chapter 7, Sims Bishop discusses the lack of attention given to literature and minorities in *BNR*. She shares her concerns about this issue and specifically focuses on the need for literature that is appropriate for minorities in their quest to extend literacy.

Herber and Nelson-Herber, in chapter 8, examine the section in *BNR* on extending literacy. They suggest that the section represents a limited perspective on the topic in its narrow interpretation of the research and practice cited and in the wide array of research and practice not cited. They define the concept of extended literacy and make a case for a comprehensive approach to content reading and reading instruction at the secondary and post-secondary levels.

A public school principal's reaction to the report is provided in chapter 9 by Wilkerson, who points out that while there is a need to incorporate many of the elements in reading instruction recommended in *BNR*, the responsibility for improvement in reading instruction resides with administrators and teachers working together. She argues that dependency on textbooks to guide instruction may be a handicap for effective teachers who are meeting the needs of individual students in their classrooms.

The final chapter, by Pinnell, addresses the possible positive and negative outcomes for curricula were *BNR*'s recommendations to be implemented. She analyzes nine recommendations and shows that each has the potential for good or poor results. She clearly shows that actions can be positive or dangerous depending upon how educational practitioners and policymakers carry out the task of implementation.

The purpose of this monograph is to continue the dialogue about reading and the reading process. Only by examining the full variety of perspectives about critical issues in reading, examining the full scope of research on which these perspectives are based, and examining practices compatible with the theoretical constructs guiding them will we do justice to the search for truth concerning reading and reading instruction.

Jane L. Davidson
Northern Illinois University

Reference

Bennett, W. J. 1986. *What Works: Research about Teaching and Learning.* Washington, D.C.: U.S. Department of Education.

1 Reading Instruction and Underlying Metaphors in *Becoming a Nation of Readers*

David Bloome
The University of Massachusetts

Cheryl M. Cassidy, Marsha Chapman, and David Schaafsma
The University of Michigan

Becoming a Nation of Readers (Anderson et al. 1985) is one of a series of recent reports on the state of education. The accuracy of the information in these reports and the utility of their recommendations continue to be challenged and defended by researchers and practitioners.

The purpose of this chapter is to examine the underlying metaphors employed in *BNR* and their potential rhetorical consequences. As Lakoff and Johnson (1980) state,

> Metaphors may create realities for us, especially social realities. A metaphor may thus be a guide for future action. Such action will, of course, fit the metaphor. This will, in turn, reinforce the power of the metaphor to make experience coherent. In this sense metaphors can be self-fulfilling prophecies. (p. 156)

In addition Lakoff and Johnson view metaphors as potentially constituting "a license for policy change and political and economic action" (p. 156). Effecting policy change, political action, and economic action are part of the rhetorical intent of reports like *BNR*. The underlying metaphors in *BNR* need to be examined because such metaphors often go unnoticed.

Becoming a Nation of Readers consists of three essays — the foreword, the main report, and the afterword — by different authors. Although the foreword and afterword are brief, they frame how the report should be viewed by the public, thus requiring an examination of the underlying metaphors in all three essays.

For the present paper, the metaphors in *BNR* were examined by at least two people who carefully read each section and generated a list of metaphors. As Lakoff and Johnson (1980) point out, metaphors can range from elaborated descriptions to the use of a single word. We concentrated our attention on those metaphors that were (*a*) recurrent, (*b*) used as organizers for large bodies of information, or (*c*) part of a coherent set of metaphors (that is, thematically related). Other metaphors were noted, but their use was not considered as part of the analysis. Further, since space in this chapter is limited, we do not discuss all instances of the use of major metaphors. Thus, although we have carefully identified the use and location of metaphors, the discussion here should be viewed as more illustrative than definitive.

We do not view the underlying metaphors employed in *BNR* as explicit intentions. We have no knowledge about how the metaphors were chosen. Many of the metaphors used can be found throughout educational research. We do not suggest that the authors explicitly intended to communicate the concepts embedded in their metaphors. Rather, we are concerned with the potential rhetorical effect, regardless of intention.

Debates, Training, and Quality Control: The Foreword

The foreword, written by Robert Glaser, summarizes the main report. In so doing, Glaser uses three major metaphors: research as a debate, learning to read as training, and educational policy with regard to instruction as quality control.

Research as a Debate

The report, Glaser writes, "lay[s] to rest once and for all some of the old debates about the roles of phonics and comprehension" (p. vi). Further, "This research [synthesized in *BNR*] often supports accepted effective practices and removes them from unnecessary debate" (p. v). A debate metaphor suggests two opposing sides, each primarily concerned with winning and losing. From this perspective, the "truth" lies with the side that can argue more effectively and present more and more important arguments for its view. As such, to find truth one merely adds up how many points each side has scored based on quantity and importance of information and then declares the winner. Once a winner is declared, the losers and the issues and facts they raised can be dismissed and ignored. The winners get the trophy, which in the area of reading may be grants, ability to influence public educational policy, and consultantships for school systems and basal reading programs.

Questions need to be asked about the appropriateness of a debate metaphor to describe research. Researchers need to account for all of the information and insights generated about a topic such as early reading development and instruction. One cannot (or should not) dismiss issues, findings, perspectives, or facts because they do not fit with one's particular advocacy. Researchers do not (or should not) organize themselves into opposing sides concerned about winning and losing; rather, they are concerned about accounting for the information gathered about a particular topic in a coherent manner. To do so may require looking at the topic from new directions and perspectives.

Learning to Read as Training

Glaser writes, "We can think of literacy as an acquired proficiency. Like achieving high levels of competence in swimming or in playing a musical instrument, competence in reading requires appropriate conditions and long periods of training" (p. vi). Comparing reading to swimming and playing a musical instrument suggests the following: (*a*) reading is primarily the activity of an individual; (*b*) reading development occurs through practice; and (*c*) reading development is similar to the development of muscles, coordination, and perceptual abilities such as ear training. *Training* also suggests the need for a regimen of practice that is frequently, if not always, painful or at least unpleasant. A training metaphor provokes an image of "no pain, no gain."

Questions need to be raised about the use of a training metaphor. Reading is not necessarily an individual performance (cf. Heath 1983; Cazden 1981), nor does its acquisition need to be unpleasant. Practice, as in practicing the 100-meter freestyle (e.g., doing the same thing over and over) or practicing the violin (e.g., rehearsing a few notes until perfection, rehearsing the next set of notes, and then finally putting them together), may not be a prerequisite for reading development. Nor is it necessarily a given that reading development should be painful, unpleasant, or boringly repetitious. Put in the jargon of reading research, the training metaphor suggests an emphasis on learning-to-read activities while not acknowledging the role of reading-to-learn and reading-to-do activities in young children's reading development.

Educational Policy as Quality Control

Glaser writes that the work synthesized in *BNR* "can secure greater reliability in instruction and render educational outcomes more predictably beneficial" (p. viii). In addition, Glaser writes that *BNR* synthesizes knowledge about and for "tests that significantly drive what is taught and learned" (p. vii). When these metaphors are viewed as a coherent whole, they suggest a standardization of reading instruction and curriculum (through testing) in order to produce a reliable and useful product. Further, educational policymakers should engage in quality control of the processes and products employed in instruction.

The quality control metaphor suggests that standardization of instruction and of the processes and products of reading instruction is beneficial. From the perspective of an administrator, standardized instructional practices and products may be more manageable, but standardization may or may not be beneficial to children. The metaphor used here subtly suggests that it *is* beneficial. Further, the metaphor suggests an input-output model of instruction: certain instructional practices (which may vary according to student characteristics and curriculum) are implemented and certain product outcomes (e.g., test scores) are derived. However, questions need to be raised about such an assumption. Recent research on teaching suggests that instruction be viewed as a complex interaction between teachers, students, and the institutional context in which they engage each other (e.g., Doyle 1983; Dunkin and Biddle 1974; Green 1983). Simply put, teachers and students react to each other and the situations in which they find themselves in unscripted (if not unique) ways. Viewing what occurs in instruction in terms of manufacturing processes or quality control may obfuscate important dimensions of instruction. Educational policy based on such metaphors (e.g., Florida's Instructional Measurement Instrument) may fail to account for key aspects of reading instruction (see Wallat 1987 for a discussion of this issue and for a critique of the Florida instrument).

Reading Development as a Journey, Instruction as Business: The Main Report

Two major metaphors may be identified throughout the main report. Reading development is often compared to a journey, and instruction is often described in the jargon of business or economics. These two metaphors play a major role in organizing information about growth in reading and instruction, and in suggesting recommendations.

Reading Development as a Journey

Anderson et al. write, "Becoming a skilled reader is a journey that involves many steps" (p. 4). Terms related to a journey reappear throughout the report: *steps, pace, progress*, etc. Terms such as *covered* (as in distance covered or words covered) and *efficient* are also incorporated into the journey metaphor.

A journey metaphor suggests a linear progression: one foot in front of the other, one step at a time. It suggests a destination: one travels to reach a particular goal. Of course, one may engage in a journey for its own sake, but that is not its usual connotation.

From the perspective of a journey metaphor, what is important is the degree to which any activity moves one toward the destination. Presumably, the destination is proficiency in reading. Yet, what constitutes proficiency in reading is not defined; rather, a common definition (or destination) is assumed. From the perspective of a journey metaphor, many kinds of travelers (students) can be presumed: those who quickly complete the journey, those who are slow, those who exert little effort to complete the journey, those who exert much effort, those who ride in limousines, those who walk barefoot, those who get lost, etc. Some travelers may need guides; others are fine without them.

The problem with a journey metaphor is that it presumes a journey — that reading proficiency is an accomplishment requiring a series of steps. While there may be several potential paths taken, the basic processes involved are going through the steps and covering ground. From this perspective, knowledge about reading development counts only if it can describe what steps to take and what paths to take to cover ground quickly.

On several occasions, Anderson et al. write that it is inaccurate to view reading development as mastery over a series of subskills. Reading is an integration of various skills employed simultaneously, and overemphasis on subskills can be detrimental to reading development. From the perspective of a journey metaphor, the point Anderson et al. make is that walking and running are more than the taking of individual steps added together. (Anderson et al. do not use the walking versus stepping metaphor). Yet, regardless of whether one is walking, running, or traveling by limousine, the quickest path is outlined in *BNR*: phonics first, then comprehension. Perhaps just as important as outlining the quickest path are the underlying assumptions that there is a quickest path, that this path can or should be taken, and that it is advantageous to do so.

There is much discussion in the reading field, however, about whether phonics first, comprehension later is the quickest path to reading proficiency. Indeed, there is discussion about whether phonics is beneficial at all to reading development. And while that discussion is important, also important is what constitutes reading proficiency and reading development. If reading proficiency is viewed as a single entity or a single, unitary set of cognitive processes, then it may be reasonable to view reading development as a journey. However, if reading proficiency is viewed as a communicative phenomenon that is simultaneously social and cognitive, varying in its organization and demands across situations, then it would be inappropriate to view reading development as a journey. From this perspective, more appropriate metaphors might include belonging to a community (Heath 1983; Cook-Gumperz, Gumperz, and Simons 1981; Hymes 1981; Robinson 1987; Bloome, Wong, and Wampah 1985), discovery (Odell 1980), and construction (Rumelhart 1980). Each of these metaphors provides a different interpretation of essentially the same "realities" described by Anderson et al. Further, each provides a different set of criteria for evaluating the worthiness and contribution of research on reading development, which also provides a different picture or view of the nature of reading development. (It should be noted that Anderson et al. *do* employ metaphors other than that of a journey to describe reading development, but none with the recurrence or coherence of the journey metaphor.)

Instruction as Business

Many of the recent reports on education have employed an economic perspective (indeed, business metaphors are often used in the education literature). *A Nation at Risk* (1983), for example, claimed that schooling and education are directly related to how well America competes economically with foreign countries, especially Japan. While such claims are probably more related to nationalism (or xenophobia) than to factual evidence, part of what is important is the use of an economics and business perspective to evaluate education.

A business or economic perspective is also employed in *BNR*. Anderson et al. write, "Economics research has established that schooling is an investment that forms human capital," and "While a country receives a good return on investment in education . . . the returns are highest from the early years of schooling when children are first learning to read" (p. 1). Terms such as *managing, management, efficient, allocated, premium, produce, standardization, performance,* and *investment* recur throughout *BNR*. A business metaphor further connotes such things as profit, labor, work, contracts, and competition. Businesses compete with each other for profit. People work for businesses and get paid for their labor. A well-run business is one that makes a profit and is efficient. Efficiency is measured by comparing the investment made with the profit returned.

One implication of a business metaphor for instruction is that participating in classroom lessons is work. Students negotiate contracts (explicit or implicit) with their teachers: they perform at a certain level and they receive a corresponding grade (cf. Doyle 1983). Students compete with each other for incentives (grades), and schools and communities compete with each other for economic opportunities based on test scores. From this perspective, it may be less important to do well in school in order to learn something, and more important to do better in school and on tests than your cohorts. A student's enjoyment of learning to read in school may not be viewed as important for its intrinsic value but rather because the student may subsequently become a more productive worker. A well-managed and efficient classroom (e.g., high time-on-task) is important because it will produce a greater profit (e.g., higher test scores) and greater economic opportunities (e.g., college entrance opportunities, higher-paying jobs).

Reading instruction can also be viewed in terms of efficiency. Instruction that maximizes higher reading achievement scores is thus desirable. Instruction that engages the students in reading activities not directly related to test scores is viewed as inefficient and wasteful, even if such activities have intrinsic value (e.g., listening to books being read aloud). Instruction, in short, should be driven by achievement tests. (Of course, the tests should measure what is important. However, what is at issue here is that it is the test itself that is important, regardless of its content.) Instruction that can be given to the largest number of students simultaneously without too great a loss of achievement is also efficient, providing a greater return for the investment made.

When instruction and classroom learning are viewed from a business or economic perspective, information is organized accordingly, as are the implications for educational policy. However, children are not raw materials to be refined and then sold for a profit. Reading competence is not (or should not be) an attribute acquired to make a child more marketable to employers. True, for many businesses, an employee with competence in literacy skills is more valuable. It is also true that students desire to have employment opportunities available to them. Yet, children and students are not reducible to marketable objects like so many mannequins or toy robots, nor is literacy reducible to the enhanced packaging of a marketable object like flashing lights on a toy robot. Literacy education, in short, is simply not reducible to the needs and demands of business and industry.

Educational policymakers, from the secretary of education to school board members to superintendents to principals to teachers, need to be very cautious about what set of metaphors they use to organize their thinking about reading and reading instruction. As discussed earlier, there are alternative metaphors and alternative ways of viewing reading instruction. Each metaphor has policy implications and consequences.

Reading Problems as a Disease: The Afterword

The afterword to *BNR,* written by Jeanne Chall, is primarily concerned with people — children and adults — who have problems learning to read. Chall does not specifically deal with the main report except to agree with its findings and to suggest that following its recommendations will improve the reading ability of all students.

The metaphor employed in the afterword compares reading problems to having a disease. Chall writes, "Many of their [reading] problems can, of course, be significantly lessened in the coming generations if the knowledge contained in this report is used wisely and well. We know from health care, however, that although prevention is essential, treatment is nonetheless needed for those already having problems" (p. 124). Words such as *diagnosis* and *remediation* tend to support the disease metaphor.

It is not our intention here to argue whether or not specific diseases do or do not affect children's learning to read; we assume that there are diseases that affect neurological functions which in turn ultimately affect learning to read. Nor is it our intention to argue what percentage of the population can be said to have a reading problem that is the result of a neurological disease. Rather, our intention is to examine the potential rhetorical consequences of viewing reading problems as a disease. We will discuss one of those potential rhetorical consequences at length. (We reiterate that we are not suggesting an intention behind the use of any particular metaphor. Rather, we are only concerned about potential rhetorical consequences that the use of a particular metaphor might have, regardless of whether such consequences were intended.)

One set of consequences of the disease metaphor might be to view the antecedents of reading problems in general as diseases. Since diseases are located in the individual, researchers and educators would look for the causes of reading failure within the individual: simply put, something is wrong with the child (or adult). A second set of consequences of the disease metaphor would be to view programmatic attempts to deal with reading problems as the treatment of a diseased individual: the child's reading problem is treated until the child is better. Programs would be organized to deal with the individual student having the problem (e.g., establishing reading clinics). A third set of consequences of the metaphor may be to view children with reading problems as coming from disease-ridden environments. Chall notes that many of the children and adults with "special problems in learning to read . . . tend to remain behind in reading and related academic subjects. . . . This group includes children from low income families, ethnic minorities, non-English or recent speakers of English, and those with specific reading and learning disabilities" (p. 123). One potential consequence of the disease metaphor might be viewing the groups listed as inherently inferior.

With regard to this third potential consequence, statistical studies show that children from low-income families and ethnic minorities (especially oppressed minorities, see Ogbu 1974) score lower on reading achievement tests than their white middle-class counterparts. However, statistical studies do not provide explanations.

A sizable amount of recent research has explored the school and family environments of low-income families and ethnic minorities (e.g., Rist 1978; Bloome and Golden 1982; Bloome, Wong, and Wampah 1985; DeStefano, Pepinsky, and Sanders 1982; Taylor and Gaines 1982; Bloome and Green 1982; Anderson and Stokes 1984; Cook-Gumperz, Gumperz, and Simons 1981; Hymes 1981; Ogbu 1974; Heath 1983; Shultz, Erickson, and Florio 1982; Trueba, Guthrie, and Au 1981; Cazden, John, and Hymes 1972; Philips 1982; Simons 1979). While an even greater number of these studies is needed, what they suggest is that the failure of children from low-income families and ethnic minorities to score higher on reading achievement tests has its roots in explicit and implicit discrimination against such children. Such discrimination may range from low expectations held by teachers and lack of appreciation for the cultural heritage children bring to school, to explicitly illegal acts of tracking ethnic-minority children into low-track and special education classes because of the dialect or language they speak, to the continued segregation and underfunding of education for children of low-income families and ethnic minorities. Discrimination against such children may also be found in the civil and social welfare resources provided (or not provided) to low-income and ethnic-minority communities (e.g., lack of access to medical service, lack of library facilities). Recent studies of the literacy environment of low-income families and ethnic minorities, including those studies conducted inside the home, provide no evidence to suggest inherent cultural or linguistic deficiencies (e.g., Anderson and Stokes 1984; Bloome and Green 1982; Bloome, Wong, and Wampah 1985; Heath 1983; Taylor and Gaines 1982). Rather, such studies have reported rich language and literacy environments. (Differences in the interpersonal organization of language and literacy activities have been found, but there is disagreement among researchers about whether such differences are directly related to differences in children's achievement in school.)

In sum, there is a series of potential rhetorical consequences in using a disease metaphor to describe reading problems. Those consequences include how reading problems are described, how they are handled, and where they are located. Using other metaphors might suggest other kinds of descriptions, programs, and locations.

Conclusion

Using metaphors in written reports may be unavoidable. Yet, the metaphors used may powerfully suggest how information is to be organized, what information is to be viewed as valid, and what courses of action should be taken. Perhaps more importantly, the use of one set of metaphors hides the relevant information, ways of organizing information, courses of action, and potential consequences that might have been suggested by the use of another set of metaphors.

With reports such as *BNR*, in which the intention is to generate changes in public policy on a broad scale, readers need to consider carefully the impact of the metaphors employed, as well as the validity of the information presented. Before educators implement recommendations from *BNR* (or any other report), they need to consider their acceptance of the underlying metaphors involved and the potential consequences of that acceptance.

Bibliography

Anderson, R., and S. Stokes. 1984. Social and Institutional Influences on the Development and Practice of Literacy. *Awakening to Literacy*, ed. H. Goelman, A. Oberg, and F. Smith. Portsmouth, N.H.: Heinemann.

Anderson, R., E. Hiebert, J. Scott, and I. Wilkinson. 1985. *Becoming a Nation of Readers: The Report of the Commission on Reading.* Washington, D.C.: National Institute of Education.

Bloome, D., and C. Golden. 1982. Literacy Learning, Classroom Processes, and Race: A Microanalytic Study of Two Desegregated Classrooms. *Journal of Black Studies* 13: 207–26.

Bloome, D., and J. Green. 1982. *Capturing the Social Contexts of Reading for Urban Black Junior High School Youth: A Sociolinguistic Ethnography.* Final report to the National Institute of Education. Washington, D.C.: U.S. Dept. of Education.

Bloome, D., L. Wong, and K. Wampah. 1985. *Locating Learning during Classroom Reading and Writing Activity.* Paper presented at meeting of the American Educational Research Association, Chicago.

Cazden, C. 1981. Social Context of Learning to Read. In *Comprehension and Teaching: Research Reviews,* ed. J. Guthrie. Newark, Del.: International Reading Association.

Cazden, C., V. John, and D. Hymes, eds. 1972. *Functions of Language in the Classroom.* New York: Teachers College Press.

Cook-Gumperz, J., J. Gumperz, and H. Simons. 1981. *School-Home Ethnography Project.* Final report to the National Institute of Education. Washington, D.C.: U.S. Dept. of Education.

DeStefano, J., H. Pepinsky, and T. Sanders. 1982. Discourse Rules for Literacy Learning in a First Grade Classroom. In *Communicating in the Classroom,* ed. L. C. Wilkinson. New York: Academic Press.

Doyle, W. 1983. Academic Work. *Review of Educational Research* 53: 159–200.

Dunkin, M., and B. Biddle. 1974. *The Study of Teaching.* New York: Holt, Rinehart & Winston.

Green, J. 1983. Exploring Classroom Discourse: Linguistic Perspectives on Teaching-Learning Processes. *Educational Psychologist* 18: 180–99.

Heath, S. 1983. *Ways with Words: Language, Life and Work in Communities and Classrooms.* New York: Cambridge University Press.

Hymes, D. 1981. *Ethnographic Monitoring of Children's Acquisition of Reading /Language Arts Skills in and out of the Classroom.* Final report to the National Institute of Education. Washington, D.C.: U.S. Dept. of Education.

Lakoff, G., and M. Johnson. 1980. *Metaphors We Live By.* Chicago: University of Chicago Press.

National Commission on Excellence in Education. 1983. *A Nation at Risk: The Imperative for Educational Reform.* Washington, D.C.: U.S. Dept. of Education.

Odell, L. 1980. Teaching Writing by Teaching the Process of Discovery: An Interdisciplinary Enterprise. In *Cognitive Processes in Writing,* ed. L. Greeg and E. Steinberg. Hillsdale, N.J.: Erlbaum.

Ogbu, J. 1974. *The Next Generation: An Ethnography of Education in an Urban Neighborhood.* New York: Academic Press.

Philips, S. 1982. *The Invisible Culture: Communication in Classroom and Community on the Warm Springs Indian Reservation.* New York: Longman.

Piestrup, A. 1973. *Black Dialect Interference and Accommodation of Reading Instruction in First Grade.* Monographs of the Language-Behavior Research Laboratory. Berkeley: University of California.

Rist, R. 1978. *The Invisible Children: School Integration in American Society.* Cambridge, Mass.: Harvard University Press.

Robinson, J. 1987. Literacy in Society: Readers and Writers in the Worlds of Discourse. In *Literacy and Schooling,* ed. D. Bloome. Norwood, N.J.: Ablex.

Rumelhart, D. 1980. Schemata: The Building Blocks of Cognition. In *Theoretical Issues in Reading Comprehension: Perspectives from Cognitive Psychology, Linguistics, Artificial Intelligence, and Education,* ed. R. Spiro, B. Bruce, and W. Brewer. Hillsdale, N.J.: Erlbaum.

Shultz, J., F. Erickson, and S. Florio. 1982. Where is the Floor? Aspects of Cultural Organization of Social Relationships in Communication at Home and at School. In *Children in and out of School,* ed. A. Glatthorn and P. Gilmore. Washington, D.C.: Center for Applied Linguistics.

Simons, H. 1979. Black Dialect, Reading Interference and Classroom Interaction. In *Theory and Practice of Early Reading, Vol. 3,* ed. L. Resnick and P. Weaver. Hillsdale, N.J.: Erlbaum.

Taylor, D., and C. Gaines. 1982. *The Cultural Context of Family Literacy.* Paper presented at meeting of the National Reading Conference, Clearwater, Florida.

Trueba, H., G. Guthrie, and K. Au. 1981. *Culture and the Bilingual Classroom: Studies in Classroom Ethnography.* Rowley, Mass.: Newbury House.

Wallat, C. 1987. Literacy, Language and Schooling: State Policy Implications. In *Literacy and Schooling,* ed. D. Bloome. Norwood, N.J.: Ablex.

2 Emerging Literacy: What We Know Should Determine What We Do

Jane L. Davidson, Doug Lia, and Cheryl R. Troyer
Northern Illinois University

[There are] children to be found now and then who learn to read for themselves, no one knows how or when. They grew into it as they learned to talk, with no special instruction or purposed method. And usually such readers are the best and most natural readers of all. (Huey, 1908, pp. 329–30)

Interest in emerging literacy has continued from the time of Huey's early observations and description of the phenomenon of children who read naturally — with no instruction. Through the years the body of knowledge has grown. The classic work done by Clay (1966, 1975, 1979) sparked additional impetus and direction in the investigations of emerging literacy; currently a rich body of knowledge exists about emerging literacy among young children.* *Becoming a Nation of Readers,* however, reflects little understanding of the importance of that knowledge in setting clear directions for continued literacy growth of children.

In *BNR*, Anderson et al. view reading as "part of a child's general language development and not as a discrete skill isolated from listening, speaking, and writing" (p. 30). Certain observations and recommendations from the report are consistent with that view; for example, providing children with a broad range of experiences and talking with them about those experiences, reading aloud to children, and providing children with opportunities and materials for writing. However, inconsistencies occur when the authors discuss parental support in fostering literacy development. They suggest that parents

---

* Notable among the research in emerging literacy are descriptive studies (Briggs and Elkind 1977; Durkin 1961, 1966; Forrester 1977; Manning and Manning 1984; Plessas and Oakes 1964; Price 1976), case studies (Baghban 1984; Bissex 1980; Butler 1979; Krippner 1963; Lass 1982, 1983; Torrey 1969), and studies from an ethnographic perspective (Bloome 1985; Clark 1976; Cochran-Smith 1984; Heath 1980; Schieffelin and Cochran-Smith 1984; Taylor 1983).

"must put their intentions into practice if their children are to have the foundation required for success in reading" (p. 28). Not only do the authors not elaborate on the subject of what *kinds* of intentions they are referring to, they do not acknowledge that adult-child interactions and the language used in the home are diverse and culturally determined events that foster literacy in a variety of ways.

Emerging Literacy: A Social Process

The role of parent-child communication in literacy development is critical (Baghban 1984; Lass 1983; Taylor 1983). The authors of *BNR* focus on only one purpose for that communication, that of imparting knowledge. Omitted is any reference to Heath's (1980) three main criteria for becoming literate: (1) that the individual have a setting or context in which there is a need to be literate, (2) that the individual be exposed to literacy, and (3) that the individual get some help from those who are already literate. The context and exposure to literacy take place in the home; the help is provided by the child's parents and significant others.

Heath's criteria are met in homes where communication abounds; for example, parent-to-parent (or significant other), parent-to-child, and child-to-child. Numerous literacy events occur — making lists, reading and writing letters, ordering from catalogs — all of which create within children a need to communicate. Reading, writing, speaking, and listening occur naturally in this kind of social environment. Children are thus afforded the opportunity "to observe written language functioning in [everyday] activities where reading and writing are involved" (Teale 1982, p. 564).

Parents provide other reading and writing experiences because they are pleasurable experiences for both parent and child and also part of what parents do almost instinctively to help children grow. Some of these activities may be ritualistic, based on traditional family customs of Bible reading or bedtime stories, and others may be child-initiated, such as taking orders in a make-believe restaurant or the child's pretending to be a reading or writing parent. Contrast these experiences with contrived models of reading and writing experiences such as those created when parents are told they should prepare their children for school in prescribed, skill-oriented ways. Artificial activities such as those in grocery store workbooks do not provide the kind of rich and complex understanding that naturally occurring literacy events do (DeFord 1981).

Reading Aloud

Most authorities would agree with the following statement from *BNR*: "The single most important activity for building the knowledge required for eventual success in reading is reading aloud to children" (p. 23). However, the purposes for such reading need to be considered. The report suggests that the child's active participation in the story-reading experience is crucial, but the definition of that active involvement with terms and phrases such as *discussions, identify letters and words, talking about the meanings of words,* and *questions similar to those that teachers ask* (p. 23) suggests a school-like involvement with text. The use of terms such as *tutor, teaching,* and *instruction* when referring to parent-child involvement implies something very different from the quality and sensitivity in family story sharing described by Taylor (1983). Book sharing that is intricately woven into the social process of family life facilitates communication between parents and children. That social process involves not only interaction between author and reader but also reader and listener. Through this highly personalized experience, children experiment with reading text and learn about the sounds of written language. Literacy then evolves as an interpersonal process, based on functional utility and demonstrated by children's most significant others — their parents and siblings.

According to research findings not discussed in *BNR*, story reading has high correlation with language development (Honig 1982; Teale 1981), vocabulary development (Cohen 1968; Teale 1981), becoming an early reader, and success in school (Freshour 1971; Teale 1981; Walker and Kuerbitz 1979). Increased competency in reading comprehension has been shown to correlate with story reading (Brown 1977; Cohen 1968; McKenzie 1977). Story reading also helps to expand children's literary language, making it possible for them to predict when they read (McKenzie 1977; Brown 1977; Teale 1981). During the process of being read to, a child learns that

> print is meaningful, that print can be turned into sound, and that written language is different from oral language. Also, in these reading events the child learns certain features of written language (as evidenced by her/his ability to mimic the lexicon, structure and prosody typical of written language). (Teale 1981, p. 903)

Other investigations have reported similar findings (Cohen 1968; Cohn 1981).

Facilitating Potential

Story reading helps children to learn the special language strategies needed to interpret storybooks, and it lays a foundation for literacy (Cochran-Smith 1984). It aids enjoyment of reading and learning the characteristics of print (Clark 1976). Story reading is also a motivational factor for young children (Clark 1976; McKenzie 1977). Clark reports that repeated readings of the same story are valuable in sensitizing children to book language, a process which she states "is probably more valuable preparation for school than any attempts at teaching a child phonics or even a basic sight vocabulary" (p. 104).

Based on what we know about the benefits and outcomes, the major reasons for story reading are as follows: parents can sensitize their children to the language of books, facilitate enjoyment, and build the predictive process necessary in meaningful reading through the natural process of story reading. Story reading, through the intimacy and social interaction of the event itself, is the means by which parents can best facilitate growth in literacy in a much more meaningful way than intentionally teaching reading "skills."

Story reading and other natural environmental events facilitate the emergence of literacy. Readiness as a set of prerequisite skills loses meaning in such a context. A child moves easily from a home environment rich in language and print to a school setting that likewise facilitates literacy learning. Unfortunately, what we know does not always govern what we do.

Adults can facilitate the child's process of internalization through story reading sessions, modeling of reading behaviors, and interaction at the level of the child's potential (Vygotsky 1978). *BNR*'s suggestion that parents "tutor preschool children in elements of reading, such as letter names" (p. 24), whether through formal means or informal ones, represents a practice that is inconsistent with the knowledge base in that such a practice reflects artificiality that is not in keeping with the development of a natural process.

Linking Writing

Children "play at" being writers just as they play at other more grown-up roles. They act as writers before they have "learned how" to write. Such play leads to the creation of structures and rules for operating with spoken and written language. The scribbles children first make to represent writing gradually give way to more accurate representations of letters and words. The seemingly random combinations of letters give way to invented spellings that gradually approach standard ones. The stories children dictate for an adult to record serve as outlets for them in their quest to make written language communicate to another (Hall 1986; Goodman 1986). Through all these approximations of what adults consider writing, children are using writing to get things done. Harste, Woodward, and Burke (1984) suggest that the most valuable gift to give young language users is to "litter their environment with enticing language opportunities and guarantee them the freedom to experiment with them" (p. 27).

Writing instruction in school should follow the lead of these natural experiences with writing. Materials and opportunities for writing should be plentiful. An environment in which children are free to take risks, and which allows experimenting with new forms and functions of writing, is crucial. Opportunities to create writing by dictating — creating the ideas and allowing someone else to record their form — encourage children to compose spontaneously, as fluently as they speak. The outcome is emerging literacy through writing as a natural environmental event.

Emerging Literacy: A Developmental Continuum

Asking the question "When should systematic reading instruction begin?" (*BNR*, p. 28) implies that such instruction should be separated from other language instruction, including writing, and should be different from the natural literacy events that have been occurring in the environments of children for the previous five years or so. According to Bloome and Holloway (1985), "What gets defined as reading and writing — whether it gets defined explicitly or implicitly — influences the nature of children's reading and writing development" (p. 40). One who looks for a point at which systematic reading and writing instruction will begin will approach the task of planning and implementing a program in a very different way from one who views literacy development as a continuum along which children progress. The constructs embedded in the typical, basal-driven approach to early reading and writing suggest that children will fit into that system in a prescribed way, that they will reach levels of mastery before progressing to the next kind of instruction, and that specific skills exist at each level of mastery. In contrast, a program of instruction based upon knowledge of how children become literate naturally views students as progressing along a developmental con-tinuum that represents the emerging processes of reading and writing. Just as the processes do not commence at a given point (unless that point is viewed as birth), they are never completed or mastered. Solidly based philosophies about the development of children and theoretical constructs about literacy should determine practices. When recommended practices are inconsistent with those constructs, chil-dren's natural progress along the continuum is diverted.

What We Should Do

Anderson et al. (1985) indicate that there is

> a wealth of evidence that children can benefit from early reading and language instruction in preschool and kindergar-ten. . . . [T]he best short-term results are obtained from pro-grams that can be characterized as formal, structured, and intensive, though whether these programs have greater long-term benefits is less clear. (p. 29)

These conclusions were drawn from studies in which success in reading was equated with high scores on formal tests. If formal, traditional readiness measures are used, then the "best short-term results" can logically be expected to come from formal, traditional programs. If, however, informal print awareness (Clay 1979) or "kidwatching" (Goodman 1978) measures are used to evaluate chil-dren's development of literacy, a more realistic picture of what children are actually able to *do* with reading and writing might be revealed.

If the wealth of evidence about the process of emerging literacy had been used as a foundation for recommended instructional pro-grams, the authors of *BNR* probably would have come to the same conclusions as the combined committees from seven major profes-sional organizations who passed a joint resolution in 1977. The resolution expressed concern about formal instruction and making decisions on economic and political bases instead of on the basis of knowledge of young children. These concerns and the recommen-dations designed to alleviate them were updated in 1986 (Early Childhood and Literacy Development Committee of the IRA, 1986) and clearly reflect the vast body of knowledge in emergent literacy. The recommendations include the following eight from a total of fifteen:

Build instruction on what the child already knows about oral language, reading and writing. Focus on meaningful experiences and meaningful language rather than merely on isolated skill development.

Respect the language the child brings to school, and use it as a base for language and literacy activities.

Ensure feelings of success for all children, helping them see themselves as people who can enjoy exploring oral and written language.

Provide reading experiences as an integrated part of the broader communication process, which includes speaking, listening and writing, as well as other communication systems such as art, math and music.

Encourage children's first attempts at writing without concern for the proper formation of letters or correct conventional spelling.

Encourage risk-taking in first attempts at reading and writing and accept what appear to be errors as part of children's natural patterns of growth and development.

Alert parents to the limitations of formal assessments and standardized tests of pre-first graders' reading and writing skills.

Encourage children to be active participants in the learning process rather than passive recipients of knowledge, by using activities that allow for experimentation with talking, listening, writing, and reading. (pp. 820–21)

The formal, structured, and intensive instruction called for by Anderson et al. has as a reference Becker and Engelmann's (1978) study involving Direct Instruction, a behavioristic program that fragments the reading process and does the very thing that Anderson et al. would not recommend — places children in a program without regard for their individual differences and advances them bit by bit through the program based on their test scores. We can only speculate whether the *BNR* recommendations were based on the following line of reasoning: if children do well, based on their test scores, in intensive formal instruction, and if they need to be prepared to meet the demands outlined in a formal basal program in first grade, then parents should "put their intentions into practice if their children are to have the foundation required for success in reading" (p. 28). In other words, if children need to fit a formal, structured program, parents must provide them with the appropriate background to succeed in that program, and their achievement will be judged according to how well they do through testing. The most disturbing note is that intensive formal instruction is totally inconsistent with the concept of emerging literacy. Such formal instruction may lead to the very "academic bootcamps" (p. 30) that Anderson et al. advise us to avoid.

Conclusion

The portions of the *BNR* "Emerging Literacy" section that are based on what is known about how children learn to read and write are appropriate and on target. The whole of that section, however, is disturbing since its conclusions about appropriate types of programs and certain ways of preparing children to enter those programs are inconsistent with the very concept of emerging literacy. In contrast, child-centered, language-based programs such as whole language programs, language-experience programs, and variations of the two *are* consistent with the concept of emerging literacy and the recommendations of the IRA Early Childhood and Literacy Development Committee. Research evidence of the success of these programs is available, and those results provide us with clear direction for curriculum planning. We must not continue to get lost in the maze of materials and commercial programs. We must continually focus on our knowledge of children, their needs, and their development in the quest for a literate society.

Bibliography

Anderson R., E. Hiebert, J. Scott, and I. Wilkinson. 1985. *Becoming a Nation of Readers.* Washington, D.C.: National Institute of Education.

Baghban, M. 1984. *Our Daughter Learns to Read and Write.* Newark, Del.: International Reading Association.

Becker, W., and S. Engelmann. 1978. *Analysis of Achievement Data on Six Cohorts of Low-Income Children from 20 School Districts in the University of Oregon Direct Instruction Follow Through Model.* Follow Through Project, Technical Report No. 78-1. Eugene: University of Oregon.

Bissex, G. 1980. *GNYS at WRK: A Child Learns to Write and Read.* Cambridge, Mass.: Harvard University Press.

Bloome, D. 1985. Bedtime Story Reading as a Social Process. In *Issues in Literacy: A Research Perspective* (34th NRC Yearbook), ed. J. Niles and R. Lalik. Rochester, N.Y.: National Reading Conference.

Bloome, D., and K. Holloway. 1985. *Early Childhood and Literacy Development.* Unpublished manuscript. Ann Arbor: University of Michigan.

Briggs, C., and D. Elkind. 1977. Characteristics of Early Readers. *Perceptual and Motor Skills* 44: 1231–37.

Brown, G. 1977. Development of Story in Children's Reading and Writing. *Theory into Practice* 16: 357–62.

Butler, D. 1979. *Cushla and Her Books.* London: Hodder and Stoughton.

Clark, M. 1976. *Young Fluent Readers.* London: Heinemann.

Clay, M. 1966. *Emergent Reading Behavior.* Unpublished doctoral dissertation. Auckland, New Zealand: University of Auckland.

———. 1975. *What Did I Write?* New York: International Publications Service.

———. 1979. *Reading: The Patterning of Complex Behavior.* 2nd ed. Exeter, N.H.: Heinemann.

Cochran-Smith, M. 1984. *The Making of a Reader.* Norwood, N.J.: Ablex.

Cohen, D. 1968. The Effect of Literature on Vocabulary and Reading Achievement. *Elementary English* 45: 209–13, 217.

Cohn, M. 1981. Observations of Learning to Read and Write Naturally. *Language Arts* 58: 549–56.

DeFord, D. 1981. Literacy: Reading, Writing, and Other Essentials. *Language Arts* 58: 652–58.

Durkin, D. 1961. Children Who Learned to Read at Home. *Elementary School Journal* 62: 15–18.

———. 1966. *Children Who Read Early.* New York: Teachers College Press.

Early Childhoood and Literacy Development Committee of the International Reading Association. 1986. Joint Statement on Literacy Development and Pre-First Grade. *Reading Teacher* 38: 819–21.

Forrester, A. 1977. What Teachers Can Learn from Natural Readers. *Reading Teacher* 31: 160–66.

Freshour, F. 1971. Parent Education and Reading Readiness and Achievement. *Reading Teacher* 24: 763–69.

Goodman, K. 1986. *What's Whole in Whole Language?* Portsmouth, N.H.: Heinemann.

Goodman, Y. 1978. Kid Watching: An Alternative to Testing. *National Elementary Principal* 57: 41–45.

Hall, M. 1986. Teaching and Language Centered Programs. In *Roles in Literacy Learning,* ed. D. Tovey and J. Kerber. Newark, Del.: International Reading Association.

Harste, J., V. Woodward, and C. Burke. 1984. *Language Stories and Literacy Lessons.* Portsmouth, N.H.: Heinemann.

Heath, S. 1980. The Functions and Uses of Literacy. *Journal of Communication* Winter: 123–33.

Honig, A. 1982. Language Environments for Young Children. *Young Children* 38: 5667.

Huey, E. 1908. *The Psychology and Pedagogy of Reading.* New York: Macmillan.

Krippner, S. 1963. The Boy Who Read at Eighteen Months. *Exceptional Children* 30: 105–9.

Lass, B. 1982. Portrait of My Son as an Early Reader. *Reading Teacher* 36: 20–28.

————. 1983. Portrait of My Son as an Early Reader II. *Reading Teacher* 36: 508–15.

McKenzie, M. 1977. The Beginnings of Literacy. *Theory into Practice* 16: 316-24.

Manning, M., and G. Manning. 1984. Early Readers and Nonreaders from Low Socioeconomic Environments: What Their Parents Report. *Reading Teacher* 38: 32–34.

Plessas, G., and C. Oakes. 1964. Prereading Experiences of Selected Early Readers. *Reading Teacher* 17: 241–45.

Price, E. 1976. How Thirty Gifted Children Learned to Read. *Reading Teacher* 30: 44–48.

Schieffelin, B., and M. Cochran-Smith. 1984. Learning to Read Culturally: Literacy before Schooling. In *Awakening to Literacy*, ed. H. Goelman, A. Oberg, and F. Smith. London: Heinemann.

Taylor, D. 1983. *Family Literacy.* Exeter, N.H.: Heinemann.

Teale, W. 1978. Positive Environments for Learning to Read: What Studies of Early Readers Tell Us. *Language Arts* 55: 922–32.

————. 1981. Parents Reading to Their Children: What We Know and Need to Know. *Language Arts* 58: 902–12.

————. 1982. Toward a Theory of How Children Learn to Read and Write Naturally. *Language Arts* 59: 555–70.

Torrey, J. 1969. Learning to Read without a Teacher: A Case Study. *Elementary English* 46: 550–56, 658.

Vygotsky, L. 1978. *Mind in Society.* Cambridge, Mass.: Harvard University Press.

Walker, G., and I. Kuerbitz. 1979. Reading to Preschoolers as an Aid to Successful Beginning Reading. *Reading Improvement* 16: 149–54.

3 Nonmainstream Groups: Questions and Research Directions

Jerrie Cobb Scott
Central State University
Wilberforce, Ohio

The ultimate influence of *Becoming a Nation of Readers* depends upon the meaning and applications that the literate community constructs from the text. Of particular importance are the implications for nonmainstream groups. If these groups are to participate in the effort to increase our nation's literacy level, questions must be answered about how the language and literacy developed within communities of nonmainstream groups facilitate the development of school literacy. Further, the answers must be utilized in designing instructional programs.

The chapter entitled "Emerging Literacy" in *BNR* speaks most directly to the issue of relationships between language and literacy in the home and in the school, an issue often found in discussion of school failure of minorities. This chapter details "the critical first steps in learning to read" (p. 21), describes "the role played by experience with reading and language in the home" (p. 21), and examines reading instruction in the early years of school. The present paper identifies questions and research directions pertinent to the acquisition of literacy in the home and in the school by nonmainstream groups.

Literacy Acquisition in the Home

BNR reminds us that literacy begins at home: "To a greater or lesser degree, depending upon the home, children acquire knowledge before coming to school that lays the foundation for reading" (p. 21). The home provides "concepts for understanding things, events, thoughts, and feelings, and the oral language vocabulary for expressing these concepts" (p. 21). Children acquire "the basic grammar of oral language" as well as specific knowledge about written language; for

27

example, "the forms of stories" and "how to recognize . . . letters and words" (p. 21). The kinds of experiences and knowledge that make for success in learning to read are also identified in *BNR*: "Children who have gone on trips, walked in parks, and gone to zoos and museums will have more background knowledge relevant to school learning than children who have not had these experiences" (p. 22).

Though not exclusive to any particular group, the kinds of experiences identified in *BNR* are likely to be encountered less frequently by nonmainstream groups than by mainstream groups. Three major questions emerge in regard to such experiences:

1. How much must home experiences and school experiences match in order to facilitate schooling?

2. Must the home experience be forced to change or can school experiences be changed to accommodate diverse experiences from the home?

3. Which nonmainstream experiences have relevance for facilitating literacy but have not been identified or recognized?

Besides special kinds of experiences, *BNR* also notes specific examples of the types of talk that some current research shows to be important: provocative questions, explanations of events removed from the here and now, complete descriptions, and complete stories. According to *BNR*, the value of these types of talk is directly related to helping children exercise their memory, reflect upon experiences, and learn how to construct meaning from events. However, there is no mention of the value of certain forms of language used in nonmainstream communities in facilitating the development of school literacy. For example, an investigation of Afro-American youth (Delain, Pearson, and Anderson 1985) explored black youths' experiences with figurative language outside of school. The researchers found that skills in sounding, "playing the dozens," and "capping" significantly influenced figurative language comprehension. They suggested that "skills acquired in the 'streets' . . . do transfer to school settings" and, further, that "teachers need to develop a respect for, rather than a bias against, the use of such language" (p. 171; see also Smitherman 1977). In short, we need more research on the facilitative effects of nonmainstream experiences on the development of school literacy.

Oral storytelling, once practiced more widely than reading stories to children, also has educational value. Obviously oral storytelling does not meet the *BNR* criteria of exposure to print language and the talk that accompanies such exposure; e.g., naming letters, matching letters and sounds, and identifying words. However, there is a long tradition of oral storytelling in many nonmainstream cultures. It can serve as useful preparation for the comprehension of written text and, in general, for acquiring a sense of story. Some studies of orality and literacy (Scribner and Cole 1978; Tannen 1984; Scollon and Scollon 1979; Akinasso 1982) offer promising new directions for understanding the educational value of oral discourse. Despite this progress, however, not enough is yet known about how predominantly oral patterns correspond to the competencies underlying reading, thus leaving many cultural groups with little or no understanding as to which of these patterns must be restored and preserved.

BNR also recommends that parents' informal teaching be centered around school-like activities. However, there is no obvious reason why peer interactions would not serve some of the same functions as parent-child interaction. For example, "playing school" is a popular game among children. The educational value of this game warrants further investigation. The research question would be "Do peer-group interactions in the context of playschool serve as a successful substitute for parent-child interactions in the facilitation of emerging literacy?"

Literacy Acquisition in the School

"Reading instruction builds especially on oral language," notes *BNR*. "If this foundation is weak, progress in reading will be slow and uncertain" (p. 30). This view points specifically to the need for more research on children's readiness for formal reading instruction. Many will recall the heated debate of the 1970s over when formal reading instruction should begin for the so-called dialect different or language-impoverished child. Many held that reading instruction should be delayed until the child has a command of standard English grammar. Their rationale was that "dialect interference" created a mismatch between students' spoken language and the standard English structures used in textbooks, thus placing an extra burden on the students' decoding processes. In only a few isolated cases, however, was the related issue of *instructional* interference treated.

Instructional Interference and Dialect Differences

As an example of instructional interference, consider the following description of a lesson in rhyming words. This description illustrates the problems that nonstandard-dialect speakers face in developing reading strategies.

> I (teacher) write the world *old* on the board. I ask a child to say it. *"Ole,"* he says. "That's right, *old.* Now give me some words that rhyme with it." *"Tole."* I know my children don't mean *toll,* so I say "Good," and write *told* on the board. *"Fole?"* I record *fold. "Bole?"* "Use it in a sentence." "I ate a *bowl* of cereal." (Channing 1968, p. 10)

The lesson continues, with the students' responses alternating between words ending with the sounds of *l* and *ld* and spelled with *le* and *ld.* Sometimes the responses are accepted; other times they are rejected. The students readjust their strategies in accordance with the teacher's rejections. They begin to offer words that begin with *o* and end with *d,* the beginning and ending sounds given in the stimulus word *old.* Finally, the teacher is bombarded with wild guesses. The teacher becomes confused, and the students rapidly lose faith in the phonics system as a decoding strategy.

For these Afro-American students, analogical reasoning sometimes yields the correct response but fails to work at other times. Phonics has failed them, as have the meanings of certain instructional terms — *rhyming words, beginning sounds,* and *final sounds of words.* More important than the lack of letter-sound correspondence, however, is the students' failure to develop dependable decoding strategies. Therefore, instructional strategies must be explored in light of what they require of students and in light of how those requirements mesh with the language patterns of the students. In addition, teachers need to understand the features of the students' dialect. More information is also needed about the decoding strategies of successful nonmainstream readers who speak nonstandard English.

In addition, instructional interference needs to be considered within the context of instructional goals. Goodman and Buck (1973) pointed out that persistent corrections of dialect miscues (deviations from written text that correspond to a child's spoken representation of the same meaning) interfered with meaning more than the structural features of the dialect did. This type of instructional interference may reflect teachers' attempts to teach standard English instead of reading; teachers have lost sight of the differences between the two. Moreover, the learner's failure to speak standard English may even be seen as failure in reading. Goodman and Buck's advice to teachers is to allow students to read in their own dialect. The instructional goal of reading is *meaning,* not the reproduction of speech.

Instructional Interference and Cultural Differences

Instructional interference also needs to be addressed in terms of textbooks. Schools could change or modify materials so that the content includes experiences and knowledge familiar both to nonmainstream groups and mainstream groups. However, research is needed to determine just how content that reflects the experiences of nonmainstream students affects these students' reading performance. Clearly, content must reflect a wide variety of nonmainstream experiences. Although publishing companies have tried to do a better job of selecting such materials than they have in past years, the results are far from adequate. Teacher's manuals also need to contain materials and techniques that reflect recognition and knowledge of the diversity of cultural differences.

Further, teacher-preparation programs in educational institutions must focus more on preparing future teachers to work with nonmainstream groups. Too many future teachers lack the necessary background knowledge and direct experiences of working with nonmainstream groups to adequately prepare them for meeting the instructional needs of these groups. Universities have an educational imperative to increase the number of persons from nonmainstream groups in teacher-preparation programs in order to alleviate some of the instructional interference that results from lack of understanding of cultural differences. In short, research needs to focus on both preservice and inservice programs designed to build understanding of cultural differences as they apply to classroom instruction.

Conclusion

The goal of becoming a nation of readers is a critical one in our society. However, the omission of recommendations in *BNR* concerning nonmainstream groups represents a serious lack of attention to a large part of our society. Research needs to focus on the oral uses of language, as opposed to written only, and on informal teaching among children, as opposed to that between parents and children only. It should be directed toward identifying the educational value of these activities for nonmainstream students. The growing interest in collaboration between researchers and teachers may assist in achieving the balanced perspective needed to produce more effective textbooks, to develop more efficient teaching methods, and to add to the body of knowledge on literacy. These are critical areas of study that must be investigated in order to facilitate the attainment of high levels of literacy for all groups in our society.

References

Anderson, R., E. Hiebert, J. Scott, and I. Wilkinson. 1985. *Becoming a Nation of Readers*. Washington, D.C.: National Institute of Education.

Akinasso, F. 1982. The Literate Writes and the Nonliterate Chants: Written Language and Ritual Communication in Sociolinguistic Perspective. In *Linguistics and Literacy*, ed. W. Frawley. New York: Plenum.

Channing, G. 1968. Bulljive — Language Teaching in a Harlem School. *The Urban Review* 2: 2–4.

Delain, M., P. Pearson, and R. Anderson. 1985. Reading Comprehension and Creativity in Black Language Use: You Stand to Gain by Playing the Sounding Game. *American Educational Research Journal* 22: 155–73.

Goodman, K., and C. Buck. 1973. Dialect Barriers to Reading Comprehension Revisited. *The Reading Teacher* 27, no. 1: 6–12.

Scollon, R., and S. Scollon. 1979. *Literacy as Interethnic Communication: An Athabaskan Case*. Sociolinguistics Working Papers No. 59. Austin, Tex.: Southwest Educational Developmental Laboratory.

Scribner, S., and M. Cole. 1978. Unpackaging Literacy. *Social Science Information* 17: 19–40.

Smitherman, G. 1986. *Talkin and Testifyin: The Language of Black America*. Detroit: Wayne State University Press.

Tannen, D. 1984. Relative Focus on Involvement in Oral and Written Discourse. In *Literacy, Language and Learning: The Nature and Consequences of Reading and Writing*, ed. D. Olson. Cambridge, England: Cambridge University Press.

4 Beyond Phonics to Language-Centered Learning

MaryAnne Hall
Georgia State University

Becoming a Nation of Readers contains a number of positive statements that are a refreshing change from some other reports on the state of American education. Teachers, teacher educators, administrators, and parents will undoubtedly applaud certain recommendations. Increasing attention to comprehension, having students spend more time writing and reading independently, providing administrative support for teachers, and lessening the amount of time pupils spend on completing workbooks and worksheets are certainly sound — if not new — recommendations. *BNR* may serve as a catalyst for renewed discussion of reading programs throughout the country. Thoughtful analysis of the report, rather than automatic acclaim for and acceptance of its content, can contribute to the improvement and enrichment of educational experiences for today's students. Certainly the title conveys a worthy aim — one that all of us in reading and in teacher education have worked toward and one that we will continue to support.

This chapter focuses on the portions of *Becoming a Nation of Readers* that deal with word identification and phonics instruction. These portions, appearing in the "Emerging Literacy" section, are among the most controversial in the discussions that the report has generated. The two recommendations "Teachers of beginning reading [through second grade] should present well-designed phonics instruction" and "Reading primers should be interesting, comprehensive, and give children opportunities to apply phonics" (p. 118) are of special concern, as is the support of intensive synthetic phonics.

Questioning Phonics in Beginning Reading Instruction

Included in the discussion about phonics is the maxim "Do it early" (p. 43). How early? Visits to nursery schools and day-care programs as well as kindergartens show that attention to phonics does indeed begin early. In a number of pre-first-grade programs, time is given every day to practice on isolated sounds or to saying "the sounds the letters make." It is linguistically inaccurate to state that letters make sounds, since letters are only representations of phonemes. Linguistic accuracy aside, however, why do children at ages three, four, and five need so much drill on phoneme-grapheme correspondence before there is any need for such knowledge? Using phonics to analyze unknown words is the apparent justification for teaching it, but before children read there is no need for this application. Having instruction in phonics completed by the end of second grade, as recommended in *BNR*, seems reasonable. It's what happens from the time of the initiation of phonics instruction to the time of leaving it behind as an instructional priority that distorts learning to read for so many children.

In *BNR*, phonics seems to be equated with word analysis. But even those who advocate a strong word-analysis component in reading programs would remind us that word analysis includes more than phonics. The point that word analysis does not *at any level* constitute a total reading program is a crucial one. In *BNR*, phonics seems to be considered so important in the beginning stages of formal instruction that other components of reading and language learning are slighted.

A disturbing question asked in *BNR* is "How should children be taught to read words?" (p. 36). This is the wrong question. Should it not be "How should children be taught to read?" or, even better, "How do children *learn* to read?" According to the report, "Reading is the process of constructing meaning from written texts" (p. 7). In the discussion of phonics, however, the authors imply that for the beginner the task is not the construction of meaning but is instead the identification of words. Note, for example, the following in *BNR*'s discussion of the need for automaticity in decoding:

> Immature readers are sometimes unable to focus on meaning during reading because they have such a low level of decoding skill. They are directing most of their attention to sounding out words letter by letter or syllable by syllable. (p. 12)

The overall implication is that comprehension does not become important until after readers have attained a level of automaticity. Yet comprehension is at the very heart of reading, regardless of the proficiency of the reader. Why is the significance of semantic and syntactic language cues overlooked in helping beginners master the complexities of written language? For young learners, intensive phonics instruction is a sure way to convey the idea that reading is (in the words of one beginner) "getting the words right." In short, the nature of the reading process as discussed earlier in *BNR* (i.e., as a meaning-making process) is ignored in the discussion of phonics, and thus the position on beginning reading in "Emerging Literacy" is inconsistent with that in the earlier section.

Phonics instruction will probably continue to be a part of reading instruction — especially in the early grades. The specific "skills" to be taught in the phonics component of the reading curriculum are easily identified and tested. The conventional wisdom that phonics is essential for learning to read successfully is so widespread that whenever aspersions are cast on the usefulness of such instruction loud outcries follow. The understanding of reading as language processing is often not readily accepted by those who have not studied the cognitive development and language learning of young children.

The debate over the years has been — and apparently continues to be — not so much whether there is to be phonics instruction but how early and how much. Instruction that includes *some* attention to sound-letter correspondence will not be totally distasteful to most reading educators if (1) such instruction is not a prerequisite for moving to the next level in a basal reader, (2) teachers understand that children can indeed learn to read without phonics, (3) phonics is not considered the answer for either beginning or remedial reading, and (4) phonics is thought of as one backup strategy for helping with unknown words encountered in actual reading.

A number of educators who are resigned to the reality of phonics instruction are disturbed about the *extent* of phonics instruction currently in evidence in schools. In many classrooms an extreme emphasis is placed on the graphophonic system of language. Tests — particularly criterion-referenced tests and end-of-level tests that accompany reading textbooks — stress decoding skills. In school systems where teachers are not permitted to take students to higher-level books until they have achieved a specified level of mastery on those tests, phonics is given much more attention than the authors of *BNR* probably intended.

For many, many years most reading educators have advocated a balanced perspective on word analysis. In the relatively brief treatment given word analysis in *BNR*, the need for that balanced perspective is likely to be lost, especially when the view promoted by *The Great Debate* (Chall 1967) is given more credibility than a broad language-based view in which the graphophonic cue system of the language is not the starting point for beginners. The danger is that well-intentioned but uninformed people will seize upon instructional materials and procedures that downplay meaning and that deal with fragments of language, thus resulting in non-language and non-texts. Such instruction is based on the erroneous assumption that such specificity will result in good reading. It is just such instruction that makes learning to read an impossible puzzle or, at best, unpleasant drudgery for so many poor achievers. They become locked into using one cue system (the most difficult and abstract one) instead of using the three cue systems of semantics, syntax, and graphophonics in an integrated way. After extensive and intensive analysis of the reading behavior of primary readers, Clay (1979) concluded, "The skills of the average and low progress readers in these three aspects of cue gathering — grammatical, semantic and letter-sound correspondence — should be strengthened, in that order" (p. 206).

What goes by the wayside when mastery of isolated skills is a high priority? When time is spent filling in the blanks not only in basal workbooks but in supplementary phonics workbooks, what happens to time for independent reading, expressive writing, and literature experiences? The answer is that usually activities considered "enrichment" or "extension" are the first to be omitted. Literature experiences, independent reading, personal writing, and creative projects are slighted and regarded only as extras instead of being valued as substantive learning experiences based on functional uses of language.

In its "Emerging Literacy" section, *BNR* deals inadequately with children as language learners. Yet recent research has added immeasurably to understanding what young learners do as they actively engage in constructing and expressing meaning with print in realistic contexts (Harste, Woodward, and Burke 1984). The research on young children's spelling development, for example, offers an impressive body of information about how children learn the intricacies of the orthographic system — not through phonics but through extensive exploration with written language (Beers and Henderson 1977). Yet the bulk of the research cited in *BNR* seems to be test-related — particularly to tests which test narrow subskills in isolation.

It is disturbing to note that *BNR* also omits any discussion — other than a swift dismissal — of whole language programs. The only research cited in *BNR* on this matter is the reference to the First Grade Studies of the 1960s (Bond and Dykstra 1967; Dykstra 1968). Other reviews of research on the language-experience approach show very favorable results with this approach in early grades (Hall 1978; Stauffer 1976). Other than the passing reference to language-experience methodology, whole language programs are not represented in the methods-comparison research cited in *BNR*. For many years we've known that the method A versus method B research did not ask or answer questions about how reading is learned. Since the time of the First Grade Studies and Chall's (1967) report, much has been learned about literacy acquisition and the contexts for literacy by studying children's actual reading and writing behaviors and by examining the socio-psycholinguistic and cognitive nature of the reading process.

Looking toward Improvements

We now have a great body of knowledge about the learning-to-read process that should guide instructional programs for language learners. The advances in knowledge in the last twenty-five years about the nature of the reading and language-learning processes must not be ignored in reading programs. In fact, one of the statements in the opening pages of *BNR* is "The knowledge is now available to make worthwhile improvements in reading throughout the United States. If the practices seen in the classrooms of the best teachers in the best schools could be introduced everywhere, the improvements would be dramatic" (p. 3). Certainly there are numerous teachers in whole language programs who would be represented in the groups of "the best teachers in the best schools." The research data examined for *BNR*, however, appear to have been much more oriented toward narrow measures of achievement than toward ethnographic evaluation of actual engagement in reading and language learning in classroom settings. Is the model of instruction to be adopted one in which reading instruction is so standardized (and sterile) that students do indeed learn to perform quite well on end-of-level tests, the various state and local CRT tests, and standardized achievement tests? If so, then vast numbers of students in such programs have been short-changed since they still do not become readers in the sense of being those who choose to read and do read outside of the school setting. Students are also shortchanged if they are not involved in extensive writing experiences.

The effect of basal reading materials in controlling instruction is indeed immense (Shannon 1983). An important point about basal readers and reading instruction made in *BNR* is the following:

> The observation that basal reading programs "drive" reading instruction is not to be taken lightly. These programs strongly

> influence how reading is taught in American schools and what
> students read. . . . The estimates are that basal reading programs
> account for from 75 percent to 90 percent of what goes on
> during reading periods in elementary school classrooms. (p. 35)

With basals and tests controlling instruction, it is difficult for teachers
to offer enriched programs. This is especially true when teachers feel
great pressure from their administrators to conform to standard
programs in order to prepare students for the tests.

The following recommendations are offered for improving reading
and language learning programs in our schools:

*Recommendation One: Move away from rigid adherence to a single
approach and/or set of materials.*

Such a movement will require that administrators look beyond the
adoption of a set of basals as the means of having an easily explainable
reading program. A reading program cannot be equated with a set
of materials. School-system personnel charged with the teaching of
reading and language arts, as well as the overseeing of that teaching,
will need to articulate their objectives and rationale as well as identify
which materials and experiences — not only basals — will fit the
objectives and rationale.

*Recommendation Two: Teachers must be listened to and respected as
professionals when they seek to adapt and enrich instruction.*

Duffy and Roehler (1982) note that "teachers do little more than
monitor pupils as they progress through commercial reading materials" (p. 440). Frequent conversations with teachers reveal that many
would prefer to have more creative and stimulating instruction but
that numerous constraints — primarily tests and strict adherence to
a single set of materials — mitigate against enriched classroom environments. Lack of a voice in decision making is one of the top
three reasons teachers leave the profession (Futrell 1986). Teachers
must become active participants in making decisions about programs,
materials, and adaptations for the individuals they teach.

*Recommendation Three: Meaningful independent work for students should
replace the ever-present worksheets and other such isolated practice.*

Included in "meaningful independent work" can be silent reading
of self-selected library materials. If students are encouraged to pursue
projects correlated with this independent reading, the project work
would also constitute meaningful independent work. Classrooms that

offer a process approach to writing (Graves 1983; Calkins 1986) engage students in worthwhile pursuits while teachers not only monitor instruction but work with other individuals and groups. Many teachers have organized their classrooms around centers (e.g., literature centers, writing centers) and have found that centers provide a viable means of offering both practice and creative open-ended whole language activities. The attention that *BNR* gives to the problem of the excessive use of worksheets and workbooks that characterizes much of today's instruction is laudable. However, the comment that "the demand for seatwork activities is insatiable" (p. 74) is disturbing. The recommendation in *BNR* emphasizing phonics in beginning reading creates the possibility that even more seatwork will be forthcoming.

Recommendation Four: Direct instruction in phonics, when and if given, should stress application so that it will be useful to students as an aid to figuring out unknown words in context in real reading situations.

In each directed phonics lesson there should be an application stage in which students are guided — with teacher explanation, not just by doing a worksheet — toward supplying an unknown word that fits the phonics understanding being taught in a particular lesson. For example, if children are learning the phoneme-grapheme correspondence for *ch* and have listened to, looked at, and discussed how words they can already read begin or end with *ch*, they can be asked to read several sentences that contain one unknown word beginning with *ch*. The teacher can say, "You know all the words except the one that has *ch* at the beginning. What word would make sense here?" as he or she displays sentences such as the following:

A bird can make a *chirping* sound.

Chocolate candy tastes good.

Boys and girls are *children.*

Even though this instruction is narrower than that which characterizes whole language programs, it is certainly more useful than synthetic blending techniques. Never should phonics instruction comprise an entire reading lesson but only a brief part of instruction.

Recommendation Five: Word identification techniques need to be broadened from phonics to a strong acknowledgment of the significance of meaning cues.

The identification of unknown words and, more importantly, of meaning is heavily dependent on the knowledge background of the reader, along with his or her expectations and semantic and syntactic cues in the context of the reading selection. The obsession with teaching fragments of language seems to rest on the erroneous assumption that reading is first learned by processing letter-by-letter and word-by-word. The statement in *BNR* that children must have ample opportunities for applying phonics should be broadened to "children need ample opportunities for reading so that they will approach reading as the construction of meaning."

Recommendation Six: Any future reports on the status of reading and language learning and teaching should include a presentation of the merits of whole language programs.

Such a presentation should focus on the rationale for and the quality of those programs. Discussion of whole language programs can also focus on how instruction is matched to the nature of the reading and writing processes.

Conclusion

In order for schools to follow the recommendations of *Becoming a Nation of Readers* (other than those on phonics), a whole language perspective and a program built on that perspective are necessary. The report's recommendations on phonics will be easy to implement (not necessarily easy for students to follow, but easy for developers of instructional materials). Developing and promoting comprehension, wide reading, and the integration of reading with the other language arts and in content areas will require much more than do the recommendations regarding phonics instruction. Certainly in the late 1980s we must move beyond the fruitless decoding debate to education that is based on the best knowledge about language learning, to instructional settings that encourage teachers to be decision makers as they actively engage children in relevant and functional language use, and to respect for learners' language potential.

References

Beers, J., and E. Henderson. 1977. A Study of Developing Orthographic Concepts among First Graders. *Research in the Teaching of English* 11: 133–48.

Bond, G., and R. Dykstra. 1967. The Cooperative Research Program in First-Grade Reading Instruction. *Reading Research Quarterly* 2: entire issue.

Calkins, L. 1986. *The Art of Teaching Writing.* Portsmouth, N.H.: Heinemann.

Chall, J. 1967. *Learning to Read: The Great Debate.* New York: McGraw-Hill.

Clay, M. 1979. *Reading: The Patterning of Complex Behavior.* 2nd ed. Exeter, N.H.: Heinemann.

Duffy, G., and L. Roehler. 1982. Commentary: The Illusion of Instruction. *Reading Research Quarterly* 17: 438–45.

Dykstra, R. 1968. Summary of the Second-Grade Phase of the Cooperative Research Program in Primary Reading Instruction. *Reading Research Quarterly* 4: 49–70.

Futrell, M. 19 May 1986. Speech at University of Georgia, Athens, Ga.

Graves, D. 1983. *Writing: Teachers and Children at Work.* Portsmouth, N.H.: Heinemann.

Hall, M. 1978. *The Language Experience Approach for Teaching Reading: A Research Perspective.* Newark, Del.: International Reading Association.

Harste, J., V. Woodward, and C. Burke. 1984. *Language Stories and Literacy Lessons.* Portsmouth, N.H.: Heinemann.

Shannon, P. 1983. The Use of Commercial Reading Materials in American Elementary Schools. *Reading Research Quarterly* 19: 68–85.

Stauffer, R. 1976. *Action Research in L.E.A. Instructional Procedures.* Newark: University of Delaware.

5 A Question of Identity, Or "The Prince was *What?*"

Karla F. C. Holloway
North Carolina State University at Raleigh

My five-year-old daughter asked me, "What word is this?" She proceeded to spell "t-a-k-e-n." "Taken," I responded, a little surprised because I thought she knew that word. "That's what I thought," she told me, "but it doesn't make sense. Listen to this . . ." She read the following sentence to me: "The prince was so taken with Cinderella that he danced with no one else the whole night long."

Questions of identification are directly parallel to issues of comprehension in reading. Once we decide whether our goal is a "decomposition" of words and sense or a comprehension of text and ideas, our teaching strategies become focused toward one of the two perspectives. Word-comprehension strategies are different in focus and degree from word-identification skills. The difference between these strategies is the subject of this essay.

Word Identification: An Inappropriate Emphasis

Very early in *Becoming a Nation of Readers,* the authors identify the structure under which "reading" is defined. They note the "partly correct" view of reading as a "process in which the pronunciation of words gives access to their meanings" (p. 8). The incompleteness of this view of reading is resolved, the authors note, by expanding it: "In addition to obtaining information from the letters and words in a text, reading involves selecting and using knowledge about people, places, and things, and knowledge about texts and their organization" (p. 8). Although this is an important addendum, the first part of the statement is troublesome. This view of reading, that one can obtain information from letters and words, sets identification skills and comprehension strategies in opposition to each other.

Frank Smith (1979) explains the conflict between identification and comprehension by noting that recognition of a word (i.e., comprehension) is not accomplished "by sounding it out — by putting together the sounds of individual letters. . . . When we read a word we do not read letters" (p. 114). His emphatic point is that the process of sounding out letters is a relatively inefficient means of comprehension in light of eye/brain processes. He writes,

> words are recognized [by the brain] in exactly the same way that cats and dogs, cars and faces, and letters of the alphabet are recognized. Words are recognized on the basis of significant differences among alternatives, on the basis of distinctive features. We learn to recognize words by learning to distinguish them from each other. (p. 115)

Smith's view is an important one. The basic question becomes whether we look at the process of reading from the standpoint of teachers and their teaching of reading, or of readers and their reading. If we determine that our teaching strategies are based on a pedagogy that proceeds from an adult's conceptual decomposition of the reading act, then we would support the former view. If we look instead at the natural strategies of children who with motivation, exposure to language, and support (but not with direct instruction) have learned to read, then we must support the latter view. We must, in any event, acknowledge the limitations of visual/oral information and the significant contribution of information from "behind the eyes" (as Smith refers to the cognitive processes).

BNR notes that the "generally accepted current model of word identification" explains the process of decoding as something that "begins . . . as soon as even partial information has been gleaned about the letters in the word" (p. 11). This emphasis on decoding at the letter/word level of reading disregards the complexity of the meaning-making process. This process cannot be constrained to simple letter-word relations. If the goal of reading is meaning, then reading proceeds from the construction (not the decoding) of an entire text. These views, of construction versus decomposition of text, are not mutually compatible, and it is critical that, in deference to teachers' teaching strategies, we do not attempt an artificial blend of these concepts. Because English is not a polysynthetic language (like Eskimo, in which long strings of bound morphemes are connected into single words), the construction of meaning occurs not at the letter or word level but at the phrase, sentence, or even paragraph level.

Holmes (1971) underscores the need to be aware of evidence that supports a view of reading that is contrary to both letter-by-letter views of word identification and word identification itself as a prerequisite to comprehension. Just as a linguist would view the study of speech sounds without regard to meaning as an abstraction, the researcher in reading must view the isolation of letters or words as a similar abstraction. Citing the psycholinguistic evidence that our memory retains meanings, not individual words, and that even oral reproductions of sentences retain meaning in place of exact words or syntactic organization, Holmes argues effectively for meaning identification as a process prior to word or letter identification. He emphasizes, like Smith (1975, 1979), that the reader's search for meaning is a far more accurate source of information about the reading process than is the decontextualized analysis of "decoding skills." If the reader's strategy is to compose and construct, then the teaching of reading must be based on the same strategy.

BNR includes such information. Its first generalization about research of the past decade on the nature of reading is that "reading is a constructive process" (p. 9). Its second generalization is that "reading must be fluent" (p. 10). The difficulty with citing such generalizations is that they are followed with questionable interpretations of construction and fluency. Both generalizations are based on the reader's ability to use prior knowledge in order to "identify individual words" (the "foundation of fluency," according to the report) and to "break the code" in order to construct meaning. These routes to fluency and meaning construction are directly antithetical to the stated goals.

Alternatives to Word Identification

Studies that examine the processes readers use to construct meaning create a different picture of beginning readers than that depicted in *BNR*. Nonproblematic readers, like Torrey's (1969) "John" (a self-taught reader) read "not the words, but the meanings" (p. 555). The skills that are emphasized as prerequisites to reading in *BNR* (word attack, decoding, an understanding of the "alphabetic principle," and an ability to "pronounce" a word so that meaning can occur) are consequences of reading and comprehension. Torrey notes that John's knowledge of phonics and his skills at word identification were absolutely subordinate to his reading. Evidence like Torrey's, gained from that percentage of children who come to school knowing how to read, is significant in understanding the process of reading. Rather than viewing such children as learning anomalies and discounting their experiences, it may be more appropriate to view them as "teaching anomalies" and to examine our teaching methodologies in light of what these children's natural experiences tell us about the learning and teaching of reading.

Such an examination would not discount evidence from psycholinguistics that suggests a close parallel between the strategies of oral language acquisition and literacy acquisition. The important structural similarity between the processes is that the early language learner is not an imitator. Neither the organization of oral language (in which meaning is represented by a deep structure) nor the environment of spoken language (with its imperfect, variable representation of syntax, meaning, and phonology) are copied by children learning to talk. Instead, adult language becomes a source of information for the learner (Smith 1975). In a similar way, the written text is a source of information for the beginning reader. The construction of information about the text comes not from an imitation of its sounds or its words, but from an organization and routing of its meaning into a recognizable experience. Words themselves lack contextual information, and letters are even further removed from informational relevancy. The skills that a child brings to the reading process are skills that are honed and refined during the years of oral language learning. Experimenting with meaning in reading involves the same processes employed in experimenting with meaning in speech. Simply stated, you learn to talk by talking and you learn to read by reading. The strategy of fluency that *BNR* states is vital to the reading process is *not,* as Anderson et al. hold, a strategy measurable by oral proficiency. That is, the goal of reading is not to be able to read aloud with fluency. It is to be able to read silently with comprehension. The development of the latter goal is a prerequisite to the performance of the former goal.

How, then, shall a youngster learn such natural strategies? Learning to read is not a matter of simply being taught strategies that are natural and that reinforce the competencies refined during oral language learning. Children learn to read when the abilities they bring naturally to language learning are encouraged (rather than explicitly taught) during literacy learning.

Making Sense of Text

It is well to keep in mind the following materials, processes, and emphases when designing and implementing a reading curriculum.

1. Variety of Print

Surrounding children with various kinds of text — fiction and nonfiction; big books and regular-sized books; text in magazines, signs, and newspapers — makes available to the literacy learner the kind of corpus that is available to the oral language learner. Children's speech and parental speech, disembodied radio voices and strangely bodied television voices, adult voices from the familiar community and strangers' voices — all of these contribute to the linguistic corpus from which the child selects information about oral language. To duplicate this wide range of voices, a wide range of text must be made available to the child learning to read. We run the risk of making an easy task difficult when we artificially limit the text environment to the basal reader and its specially developed support materials. Faced with this small sample of text, some children will choose, however unwillingly, not to engage with that particular stimulus. Rather than assault these children with instructional practices that force their attention to the items they have rejected, we need to make more kinds of real texts available to them. In other words, when limited samples don't work, the response should be to expand the opportunities. The print that children encounter must be as daring, full, and broad as the oral language they used to learn speech.

2. The Relevance of Sharing

Sharing encourages an active response to print and provides an opportunity to extend the communicative interaction between author, text, and reader to the classroom audience. However, sharing the experience of reading is different from simply reading aloud. (Many teachers ask children to read aloud not in order to share what they're reading with others but to permit the teachers to evaluate the reading.) Sharing means that children are evaluating or exchanging interpretations of the text. Sharing may mean recording the title of the story in a learning log or telling a friend about a good part in the story. It may mean baking a cake like the one in the story or putting together an art project following printed directions. All of these activities, combined with critical observation ("kidwatching") on the part of the teacher, can satisfy both our need to evaluate and the children's need to do real reading (that is, silent reading).

3. Readers' Rules

The only rules that are important in literacy learning are those that children recognize themselves. To insist that children master rules prior to reading, that only the teacher can make them sufficiently aware of those rules, and that the rules will become "usable" through drill and repetition indicates an insufficient acknowledgment of the sense of language that children bring to the act of reading. The generalizations children intuitively make about language, whether they are about sounds or syntax, are far more valuable than the artificial ones we teach them in order to make oral reading fluent.

4. Proceeding from the Whole

Early writers often make marks on a page that may or may not resemble letters, and then proceed to "read" from them something far more extensive than the quantitatively limited marks they have made. Later they may learn to make their marks represent single idea units, and then single words (Calkins 1986). A similar natural strategy is observed for early readers. Individual units, whether letters or words, have limited significance for early readers. "Starting from sense" means starting from a phrase or sentence sequence that constitutes a unit of meaning. Later, a child may be able to deconstruct meaning units into individual words, and after that into letters or sounds.

Two ideas are important in light of this process. The first is that, for the purposes of word or letter identification, children should be the guides as to whether they are ready to deconstruct meaningful units. The second is that the teacher should be very certain of his or her goals in moving away from context and sense. (A note of caution: there are few valid reasons for forcing readers to deconstruct texts that would support the goal of making them better readers. Most reasons satisfy "instructional goals" or "evaluative procedures" and may be removed from the needs and growth of the reader. They are the ones least justifiable in attaining the goal of learning to read.)

5. Oral Language

Like formal evaluation, orality ("oral literacy") is a superficial indication of the complexity of linguistic information a child has developed. Insisting that oral language capacity must be "developed" before reading can be learned perpetuates the false and dangerous notion that reading represents speech. It also focuses attention at the surface of linguistic complexity and knowledge. Children's oral language, whether or not it matches the language of the classroom, may not match the language of the texts. Nor should it. Reading does not build upon oral language facility. Rather, it builds upon internal, deep-structure awarenesses of language. These awarenesses need not be spoken to be present any more than reading must be heard to be accomplished.

Conclusion

After I explained to my five-year-old what *taken* meant in the context of Cinderella and her prince, she proceeded to read the fairy tale. It is likely that there were more words in that story she did not know, and more that she could not readily "pronounce." But not until her enjoyment and understanding of the story had been significantly interrupted did she disengage from her reading to ask me what something meant. The identification of that word was fairly simple. What was unacceptable for the reader was its disruption of the anticipated context. When an early reader focuses on word identification enabled through letter/sound recognition, making sense of print is unfairly and unnaturally interrupted.

Finally, what is as significant as the pedagogically sound reasons for beginning with meaning instead of sounds or words are the support and acknowledgment of linguistic competency due the early reader. These child-centered courtesies are reasons enough to avoid a deconstruction of the way they have successfully learned to approach language when we teach them to read.

References

Anderson, R., E. Hiebert, J. Scott, and I. Wilkinson. 1985. *Becoming a Nation of Readers: The Report of the Commission on Reading*. Washington, D.C.: National Institute of Education.

Calkins, L. 1986. *The Art of Teaching Writing*. Portsmouth, N.H.: Heinemann.

Holmes, D. 1971. The Independence of Letter, Word, and Meaning Identification in Reading. *Reading Research Quarterly* 6: 394–415.

Smith, F. 1975. *Comprehension and Learning: A Conceptual Framework for Teachers*. New York: Holt, Rinehart & Winston.

———. 1979. *Reading without Nonsense*. New York: Teachers College Press.

Torrey, J. 1969. Learning to Read without a Teacher: A Case Study. *Elementary English* 46: 550–56.

6 Focusing on Meaning in Beginning Reading Instruction

Connie A. Bridge
University of Kentucky

Few reading experts could disagree with many of the recommendations of *Becoming a Nation of Readers*. For example, the report recommends that parents should read aloud to their children and support their continued growth as readers; readiness programs should focus on reading, writing, and oral language; reading primers should be interesting and comprehensible; teachers should devote more time to comprehension instruction and less time to workbooks and skill exercises; and children should spend more time writing and more time in independent reading. One controversial recommendation, however, pertains to the teaching of phonics. Whereas most experts agree that children need to learn letter-sound correspondences early, the controversy revolves around the manner in which this is best accomplished.

In the first part of this chapter, I will discuss why the instructional suggestions made by the authors of *BNR* regarding initial phonics instruction are inconsistent with the constructivist theory of reading they espouse and with several of their other suggestions pertaining to beginning reading. These recommendations, if implemented, would deprive children of contextual support and strip the task of learning to read of its meaningful, social nature. In the second part of the chapter, I recommend instructional practices that keep the focus of reading instruction on the meaningful nature of the reading act and discuss several research studies supporting these practices.

Inconsistency between Theory and Instructional Suggestions

One of the major problems with *BNR* is the inconsistency between the theory of reading espoused and the suggestions made for beginning reading instruction. On the one hand the authors explain and defend an interactive, constructive model of the reading process. On the other hand they suggest methods of beginning reading instruction that ignore the implications of such a model. The inconsistency is perhaps not surprising in light of the discrepant views of beginning reading instruction found in comparing the publications of one of the authors (Hiebert 1986) with the writings of some of the persons who had input into *BNR* (e.g., Beck 1981; Chall 1967). Obviously, the report is a result of major attempts at compromise between a view that "familiar print [is] the ideal content for beginning reading instruction and children's use of context clues [is] the basis for teaching them strategies to independently identify words" (Hiebert 1986, p. 73), and an opposing view that advocates early phonics instruction in order to make "grapheme-phoneme correspondence explicitly available" and to provide "an instructional strategy for blending sounds into words" (Beck 1981, p. 89).

In the section of *BNR* entitled "What Is Reading?" the authors assert that "reading is the process of constructing meaning from written texts" and that it requires "the coordination of a number of interrelated sources of information" (p. 6). The authors contrast a "bottom up" or linear-sequential view of the reading process with an interactive view. They briefly summarize the linear view of reading as a sequential process in which readers begin with letter identification, proceed to word recognition, then to sentence identification, and eventually work up to paragraph meaning and text-level understanding. Subsequently the authors point out the limitations of a linear-sequential view of reading in accounting for the role of prior knowledge and the contributions that the reader makes during the reading process. One of the five generalizations that the authors draw based upon their review of the research literature of the last decade is that "reading is a constructive process" (p. 9).

Few would dispute this characterization of the reading process; indeed, the writings of numerous researchers support just such a view of reading as a constructive, interactive process (Goodman 1976a; Just and Carpenter 1980; Rumelhart 1977; Smith 1982; Stanovich 1980). Hypotheses differ as to how the contributions of different knowledge sources interact during the reading process. However, most theorists agree that the reader has multiple sources of information available during reading. Goodman discusses three major sources: the semantic, the syntactic, and the graphophonic. Smith talks about the visual information provided by the print and the nonvisual information that is stored in the reader's brain. Although the terminology varies from theorist to theorist, all would agree that the relative contributions of the various knowledge sources vary according to factors such as text difficulty, reader ability, and prior knowledge. Smith and Goodman contend that the more nonvisual information (i.e., prior knowledge of language and the world) the reader possesses, the less attention the reader must allocate to visual information during reading. Whenever the reader is comprehending the text, he or she needs less visual information.

On the other hand, Stanovich (1980) views the interactive contributions of various knowledge sources in a somewhat different way. He theorizes that the need to rely on the semantic and syntactic support of context can have negative effects on comprehension. Whenever a reader does not possess rapid and automatic word-recognition skills, he or she must allocate more attention to context to aid in word identification; thus Stanovich contends that comprehension is hindered because the reader has less attentional capacity to devote to higher levels of the comprehension process. While agreeing that the use of context is especially helpful to poor readers in facilitating word recognition, Stanovich views poor readers' dependence on context as a negative influence on comprehension.

In a recent test of the Stanovich hypothesis with first graders reading a predictable story, Leu, DeGroff, and Simons (1986) found that, contrary to predictions based on the Stanovich model, the less proficient first graders, who relied most on contextual support, did not suffer comprehension loss and indeed were able to use the strong discourse-level context as they progressed through the story to increase their reading rate to equal that of good readers. Comprehension was equal both at the propositional level and the discourse level.

Although the authors of *BNR* subscribe to an interactive, constructivist view of reading, their recommendation to teach phonics explicitly by "isolating the sounds associated with most letters and teaching children to blend the sounds of letters together to try to identify words" (p. 42) would place children in situations in which only one knowledge source or cueing system is available. When the reader is deprived of syntactic and semantic information, then comprehension of previously processed text cannot be used to facilitate decoding of subsequent text.

Compare this situation to the assertion in *BNR* that the emphasis should always be kept on meaning during reading:

> From the very beginning children should be given *all* of the elements necessary for constructing meaning. This is important because reading at this early level is a new enterprise, and

children must be made aware that reading is always directed
toward meaning. (p. 44)

The authors state further that "once the basic relationships have
been taught, the best way to get children to refine and extend their
knowledge of letter-sound correspondences is through repeated opportunities to read" (p. 38). The key phrase here is "once the basic
relationships have been taught." Beck (1981) explains that the assumption underlying the early teaching of isolated letter sounds and
sound blending is that the fundamental goal of beginning reading
instruction is to help children learn the structural relationships
between written and spoken language. Advocates of this approach
believe that this goal is best accomplished through explicit instruction
in letter-sound correspondence rather than by arranging conditions
for the novice to behave like a "miniature skilled reader." Thus, they
feel justified in involving the child in activities such as isolating
individual letter sounds and sound blending, which differ considerably
from the normal reading task.

Advocates of a meaning-based approach, on the other hand, believe
that children learn to read by reading and that if they are given
opportunities to read meaningful, predictable materials, children can
induce for themselves the manner in which letter-sound correspondences work. Gibson and Levin (1975) also support a whole-to-part
approach to reading instruction; in their classic work, *The Psychology
of Reading,* they assert,

> The beginning reader should be given simultaneous training in
> using all three types of information [semantic, syntactic, and
> graphophonic]. . . . [When] teaching a complex task it is pref-
> erable to start training on the task itself, or a close approximation
> to it rather than giving training on each component skill inde-
> pendently and then integrating them. (p. 324)

Yet the suggestion to teach isolated letter sounds and sound
blending is essentially a part-to-whole approach and implies an adherence to a linear-sequential view of the reading process. A part-to-
whole approach is not consistent with the constructivist view of the
reading process that holds that all sources of information (semantic,
syntactic, and graphophonic) are used by readers in an integrated
fashion during reading. Teaching letter-sound correspondence in
isolation would deprive children of semantic and syntactic support
and force them to depend solely on their graphophonic knowledge,
which is severely limited during the initial stages of reading acquisition.

The authors of *BNR* are thus caught on the horns of a dilemma
that they were unable to resolve in a manner consistent with the

theory of reading that they espouse. The authors of many beginning reading series have been gored by the same bull. Essentially, the problem is this: how can children "be made aware that reading is always directed toward meaning" (Anderson et al., p. 44)? How can children "be given all of the elements necessary for constructing meaning" from the very beginning (p. 44)? How can children be given "repeated opportunities to read" (p. 38) when they are in the initial stages of reading acquisition?

I contend that these goals will certainly not be met by teaching isolated letter sounds and sound blending, nor by having children read a passage like the following, which was cited in *BNR* as giving children "a *good opportunity* [italics added] to use phonics in actual reading" (p. 46):

> Ray loads the boat.
> He says, "I'll row."
> Neal says, "We'll both row."
> They leave, and Eve rides home alone.

Earlier in the report the authors had asserted that the first selections children read should be "interesting . . ., comprehensible . . ., and instructive" (p. 43). Yet the above passage has none of these qualities. This is another instance in which the authors state an important principle that evolves naturally from a constructivist view of reading but then make a suggestion for instruction that is totally incompatible with that principle.

Instructional Recommendations That Focus on Meaning

Several recent books and articles have provided insight into ways in which beginning reading instruction can be accomplished in a manner consistent with a constructivist view of the reading process. This whole body of literature was overlooked in *BNR* except for a brief mention of whole language approaches that the authors contend work successfully in New Zealand but inconsistently in the United States. Holdaway (1979, 1986), Clay (1979) and Ashton-Warner (1971) have written eloquently about the use of whole language principles in New Zealand schools. And Bridge and Burton (1982); Bridge, Winograd, and Haley (1983); DeFord (1981); Edelsky and Draper (in press); Graves and Hansen (1983); and Milz (1980) have described American classrooms in which whole language approaches have been employed successfully. I assume these accounts were among those dismissed by the authors with the following statement: "In the hands of very skillful teachers, the results can be excellent. But the average result is indifferent when compared to approaches typical in American classrooms, at least as gauged by performance on first- and second-grade standardized reading achievement tests" (p. 45).

To support the last statement regarding indifferent results in American schools, the authors cite the twenty-year-old study of Bond and Dykstra (1967). Grundin (1985), however, questions the conclusion drawn by Anderson et al. and points out that Bond and Dykstra concluded that the language-experience approaches in their study were effective programs of instruction. These language-experience approaches had some of the same elements as, and were precursors of, modern whole language approaches. Grundin (1985) also discusses the achievement test scores of youngsters in the Bond and Dykstra study. His analysis indicates that the test scores of children in the language-experience approach compared favorably to those of youngsters taught by linguistic and basal approaches.

If the authors of *BNR* had taken into account more of the recent work on the whole language approach, what recommendations would they have made regarding beginning reading instruction that emphasizes meaning? How would these recommendations have been supported? What implications would the recommendations have for instruction? The following would be quite probable and plausible answers:

1. *Beginning reading instruction should begin with meaningful, functional texts* (Goodman 1976b; Holdaway 1986; Smith 1982). These first texts should be real texts representative of a variety of genres: storybooks, trade books, jokes, riddles, poetry, instructions, recipes, TV guides, menus, letters, environmental print, etc. Smith (1982) contends that one of the two major understandings that children must possess before they can learn to read is that print is meaningful. If children's first exposure to reading is in preprimers with highly controlled vocabulary and sentence lengths, they may find it difficult to figure out that print is meaningful and functional in their lives. Literacy acquisition is essentially a social skill and is learned most easily in communal settings characterized by social satisfactions. Holdaway (1986) sums it up nicely: "Reading and writing must deeply enhance the social well-being of potential learners if skill is to be hungrily sought" (p. 69).

2. *The first texts that children are asked to read should be highly predictable.* Predictable texts are those containing an underlying structure that enables the reader to predict the next word, line, phrase,

or episode. Several research studies have confirmed the effectiveness of using predictable materials in beginning reading instruction. In comparisons with traditional basal materials, predictable materials have facilitated children's acquisition of sight vocabulary, their comprehension, their strategies for language cue system utilization, and their rate of reading. Bridge and her associates (Bridge and Burton 1982; Bridge, Winograd, and Haley 1983) found that kindergarten and first-grade children using predictable materials learned significantly more sight words than children using traditional primers and preprimers. Several studies have demonstrated that first graders reading predictable materials are more apt to use syntactic and semantic strategies rather than rely solely on graphophonic strategies (Bridge, Winograd, and Haley 1983; DeFord 1981; Gourley 1984; Rhodes 1979).

Rhodes (1979), DeFord (1981), and Simons (1985) also found higher comprehension for more predictable stories. In a comparison of good and poor first-grade readers using a predictable text, Leu, DeGroff, and Simons (1986) found that poor readers' comprehension was equal to good readers' and that as poor readers progressed through the text, their familiarity with the discourse structure enabled them to read at the same rate as the good readers. Affective factors were also positively influenced by the use of predictable materials. The children in Rhodes' (1981) study expressed a preference for reading more predictable selections, whereas the children in the Bridge, Winograd, and Haley (1983) study who were instructed in predictable texts reported more frequently that they enjoyed reading aloud in their reading group than did children instructed with a traditional preprimer.

3. *Instruction in word-recognition skills should proceed from whole to part* (Gibson and Levin 1975). Children should first be allowed to read the entire story, rhyme, finger play, language-experience story, or other genuine text. Then the teacher can begin to draw the children's attention to specific features of the text. This step is especially important for children who do not spontaneously attend to the graphophonic characteristics of individual words. Otherwise, they may not induce for themselves the rules governing letter-sound correspondence. Cunningham (1979) and Bridge (1986) recommend a whole-to-part procedure for teaching sight vocabulary. The procedure begins with reading the entire structured language text, then proceeds to line matching and finally to word matching.

A similar sequence of steps for teaching phonics is recommended by Botel and Seaver (1984), who suggest that the teacher begin by involving the children in choral reading and language play of a selected rhyme, then move to sentence instruction, to phonics instruction, and finally to vowel and consonant patterns in individual words. Holdaway's (1979) shared book experiences also move from the teacher's reading of a complete text to involving the children in reading along in the predictable parts, and then to pointing out specific text features at the word and sentence level. Hiebert (1986) recommends a whole-to-part approach using the context of familiar environmental print to introduce letter-sound correspondences. All of these procedures keep the focus on meaningful print and provide children with semantic and syntactic support while directing their attention to the significant features of individual words and to word patterns.

4. *Children need many opportunities to read easy materials fluently.* Even young children can be encouraged to role-play themselves as readers while learning to read (Bridge 1986; Holdaway 1986; Pappas 1985). This enables them to learn to read by reading. Allington (1977) has discussed the importance of providing beginning readers and poor readers with many opportunities to read fluently in easy materials. Predictable materials enable beginning and poor readers to read fluently (Leu, DeGroff, and Simons 1985) and to role-play themselves as successful readers. Repeated readings of texts can also provide successful reading experiences (Samuels 1979). These successful experiences are vitally important in the prevention of learned helplessness, which results when children who experience repeated failures during reading instruction begin to believe that they cannot learn to read and eventually stop trying (Johnston and Winograd 1985).

5. *Beginning readers should be helped to develop strategies for monitoring their own reading for meaning.* This can begin by encouraging them to keep the focus on meaning. Whenever the children are reading and encounter an unfamiliar word, they should be encouraged to read to the end of the sentence and think of what would make sense rather than be told to "sound it out." Sounding out requires that the children focus on the word itself; thus they are stranded with only one cueing system, the graphophonic, which is their weakest system during the initial stages of learning to read. Reading to the end of the sentence keeps the focus on meaning by encouraging the use of context, thus enabling the semantic and syntactic cueing systems to supplement the limited graphophonic knowledge possessed by beginning readers.

6. Another important way to help youngsters keep the focus on meaning is to *use teacher interruption behaviors that allow opportunities for self-correction.* When youngsters make a miscue that interferes with meaning, they should be allowed to complete the sentence or paragraph before being stopped by the teacher or by other children. If they do not spontaneously self-correct the miscue at that point, then they can be stopped and asked, "Did that make sense?" The children soon get the message that print should make sense and that when it doesn't, they need to reread in order to self-correct.

Allington (1980) has found that teachers' interruption behaviors differ across low- and high-achieving reading groups. With high-achieving readers, teachers don't interrupt until the end of the page or selection and then do so with a question or comment that focuses on meaning. With low achievers, however, teachers tend to interrupt immediately when a child miscues and to ask a question or make a comment that focuses only on graphophonic information, such as "Sound it out" or "Look at the beginning of the word." Again this leaves the poor readers stranded with the weakest of their three cueing systems.

This list of recommendations is not comprehensive but can provide a framework for beginning reading instruction that emphasizes the meaningfulness of reading. If teachers (1) begin instruction with meaningful, predictable texts and relate skill instruction to these texts, (2) provide many opportunities to read fluently in easy materials, and (3) encourage children to use all three cueing systems while reading, the children should be well on their way to becoming successful readers.

Summary

In this chapter I have pointed out the inconsistency between an interactive, constructivist theory of reading and the instructional practices suggested in *Becoming a Nation of Readers* for helping children learn letter-sound correspondences. I have described alternative instructional practices for beginning reading that are compatible with a constructivist view of the reading process and that keep the focus on meaning even during the initial stages of learning. Obviously, research exists to support these beginning reading practices. Why the authors of *BNR* chose to ignore this body of research is unclear. Grundin (1985) provides an interesting analysis of the implicit criteria used by the authors for inclusion of articles in the report. Regardless, it is important for teachers of beginning reading to know that there are effective ways of helping children learn to read by reading meaningful, predictable, and functional texts that always keep the focus on meaning. Teachers do not have to resort to methods that fragment reading into meaningless parts and that are potentially confusing, especially for children who arrive at school with little familiarity with the joys and purposes of print.

Bibliography

Allington, R. 1977. If They Don't Read Much, How They Ever Gonna Get Good? *Journal of Reading* 21: 57–61.

———. 1980. Teacher Interruption Behaviors during Primary-Grade Oral Reading. *Journal of Educational Psychology* 72: 371–77.

———. 1983a. Fluency: The Neglected Reading Goal. *The Reading Teacher* 36: 556–61.

———. 1983b. The Reading Instruction Provided Readers of Differing Reading Abilities. *The Elementary School Journal* 83: 548–59.

Anderson, R., E. Hiebert, J. Scott, and I. Wilkinson. 1985. *Becoming a Nation of Readers: The Report of the Commission on Reading.* Washington, D.C.: National Institute of Education.

Ashton-Warner, S. 1971. *Teacher.* New York: Bantam Books.

Beck, I. 1981. Reading Problems and Instructional Practices. In *Reading Research: Advances in Theory and Practice,* Vol. 2, ed. G. MacKinnon and T. Waller. New York: Academic Press.

Bond, G., and R. Dykstra. 1967. The Cooperative Research Program in First-Grade Reading Instruction. *Reading Research Quarterly* 2: 5–142.

Botel, M., and J. Seaver. 1984. Phonics Revisited: Toward an Integrated Methodology. Paper presented at meeting of the Keystone State Reading Association, Hershey, Pa.

Bridge, C. 1986. Predictable Books for Beginning Readers and Writers. In *The Pursuit of Literacy: Early Reading and Writing,* ed. M. Sampson. Dubuque, Iowa: Kendall/Hunt.

Bridge, C., and B. Burton. 1982. Teaching Sight Vocabulary through Patterned Language Materials. In *New Inquiries in Reading Research and Instruction,* (31st NRC Yearbook), ed. J. Niles and L. Harris. Washington, D.C.: National Reading Conference.

Bridge, C., P. Winograd, and D. Haley. 1983. Using Predictable Materials vs. Preprimers to Teach Beginning Sight Words. *The Reading Teacher* 36: 884–91.

Chall, J. 1967. *Learning to Read: The Great Debate.* New York: McGraw-Hill.

Clay, M. 1979. *Reading: The Patterning of Complex Behavior.* 2nd ed. Exeter, N.H.: Heinemann.

Cunningham, P. 1979. Beginning Reading without Readiness: Structured Language Experience. *Reading Horizons* 19: 222–27.

DeFord, D. 1981. Literacy: Reading, Writing, and Other Essentials. *Language Arts* 58: 652–58.

Edelsky, C., and K. Draper. In press. Reading/"Reading," Writing/"Writing," Text/"Text." In *Reading and Writing: Theory and Research*, ed. A. Petrosky. New York: Ablex.

Gibson, E., and H. Levin. 1975. *The Psychology of Reading*. Cambridge, Mass.: The MIT Press.

Goodman, K. 1976a. Behind the Eye: What Happens in Reading. In *Theoretical Models and Processes in Reading*, 2nd ed., ed. H. Singer and R. Ruddell. Newark, Del.: International Reading Association.

———. 1976b. *Reading: A Conversation with Kenneth Goodman*. Glenview, Ill.: Scott, Foresman.

Gourley, J. 1984. Discourse Structure: Expectations of Beginning Readers and Readability of Text. *Journal of Reading Behavior* 16: 169–88.

Graves, D. and J. Hansen. 1983. The Author's Chair. *Language Arts* 60: 176–83.

Grundin, H. 1985. A Commission of Selective Readers: A Critique of *Becoming a Nation of Readers*. *The Reading Teacher* 39: 262–66.

Hiebert, E. 1986. Using Environmental Print in Beginning Reading Instruction. In *The Pursuit of Literacy: Early Reading and Writing*, ed. M. Sampson. Dubuque, Iowa: Kendall/Hunt.

Holdaway, D. 1979. *The Foundations of Literacy*. New York: Ashton Scholastic.

———. 1986. The Structure of Natural Language as a Basis for Literacy Instruction. In *The Pursuit of Literacy: Early Reading and Writing*, ed. M. Sampson. Dubuque, Iowa: Kendall/Hunt.

Johnston, P., and P. Winograd. 1985. Passive Failure in Reading. *Journal of Reading Behavior* 17: 279–301.

Just, M., and P. Carpenter. 1980. A Theory of Reading: From Eye Fixations to Comprehension. *Psychological Review* 87: 329–54.

Leu, D., L. DeGroff, and H. Simons. 1986. Predictable Texts and Interactive-Compensatory Hypotheses: Evaluating Individual Differences in Reading Ability, Context Use, and Comprehension. *Journal of Educational Psychology* 78: 347–52.

Milz, V. 1980. The Comprehension-Centered Classroom. In *Reading Comprehension: Resource Guide*, ed. B. Farr and D. Strickler. Bloomington, Ind.: Indiana University.

Pappas, C. 1985. Learning to Read by Reading: Learning How to Extend the Functional Aspects of Reading. Paper presented at the Twelfth International Systemics Workshop, Ann Arbor, Mich.

Rhodes, L. 1979. Comprehension and Predictability: An Analysis of Beginning Reading Materials. In *New Perspectives on Comprehension*, ed. J. C. Harste and R. F. Carey. Bloomington, Ind.: Indiana University School of Education.

———. 1981. I Can Read! Predictable Books as Resources for Reading and Writing Instruction. *The Reading Teacher* 34: 511–19.

Rumelhart, D. 1977. Toward an Interactive Model of Reading. In *Attention and Performance*, ed. S. Dornic. Hillsdale, N.J.: Erlbaum.

Samuels, S. 1979. The Method of Repeated Readings. *The Reading Teacher* 32: 403–8.

Simons, H. 1985. Is Primerese Easy or Hard to Read? A Comparison of Controlled Basal Stories and More Natural Written Language Stories. Paper presented at meeting of the National Reading Conference, San Diego, Calif.

Smith, F. 1982. *Understanding Reading.* 3rd ed. New York: CBS College Publishing.

Stanovich, K. 1980. Toward an Interactive-Compensatory Model of Individual Differences in the Development of Reading Fluency. *Reading Research Quarterly* 16: 32–71.

7 The Treatment of Literature and Minorities in *Becoming a Nation of Readers*

Rudine Sims Bishop
The Ohio State University

Becoming a Nation of Readers, first of all, reflects the false dichotomy between reading and literature that is very familiar to those of us concerned with elementary language arts education. Reading is treated as its own enterprise, a separate field supported by a whole industry of textbook writers and publishers, researchers, teachers of reading, and teachers of teachers of reading. Interestingly, the logical *content* involved in reading — literature in all its variety — is usually treated separately as something else again.

BNR, then, is concerned very much with reading, and not very much with literature. It purports to synthesize current knowledge in three areas: the reading process, the teaching of reading, and "environmental influences on reading." From the perspective of someone interested in literature, the chapter on the reading process ("What Is Reading?") is somewhat limited in its scope. It does not address the growing research on response to literature, not even Louise Rosenblatt's (1978) transactional model of the process. This is an important omission because the research on response has something important to say about how individuals are affected by what they are reading. The transactional model suggests that the meaning a reader makes of a text is influenced by what he or she brings to the text. In the case of minority students, this becomes a particularly important consideration because to the extent that the experiences they bring to a text differ from those of the teacher, the meanings they make may diverge from the teacher's interpretation. Such divergences do not fare well in the many classrooms where one-right-answer questions predominate. The transactional model also implies that it could be important to include in the curriculum literature that reflects the experiences — including the cultural experiences — of the readers. In the other two areas addressed in *BNR* — the teaching of reading and environmental influences on reading — there is some attention paid to literature, though not nearly the emphasis one might expect in a monograph with something to say about the teaching of reading.

BNR not only gives literature short shrift; it gives precious little attention to minorities, even in places where such attention might be logical, such as in the discussion of ability grouping. Yet it is common knowledge that minority children, particularly those from low-income families, are more likely than their more privileged peers to end up in low-ability groups. To their credit, the authors of the report *do* recognize the negative effects of ability grouping on those who are in the low groups. However, the failure to deal more directly with the fate of minorities in our reading programs is an important weakness of the report, especially given the expected large increase in minorities in the school population over the next few decades.

When it comes to literature and minorities, we are left, then, to draw implications from bits and pieces of the report and from the major recommendations listed at the end. I have chosen to react to the summary recommendations that seem to have particular relevance to minorities and literature.

"Children should spend less time completing workbooks and skill sheets" (p. 119).

Possibly the only thing that could have made this a better recommendation is to have suggested that we do away with workbooks and skill sheets altogether. The report points out the inordinate amounts of time spent on worksheets and workbooks, as well as the dubious value of many of those exercises. While such exercises are ubiquitous, it is too often the case that students who are in the lowest ability groups — often minorities — are the ones who are deemed to need the most work on skills. Thus they tend to have much of their reading instruction time taken up with trying to learn "reading skills," and not nearly enough given over to practicing actual reading. If time spent on workbooks and skill sheets were to be greatly reduced or eliminated, and replaced with meaningful reading and writing experiences accompanied by timely and useful reading instruction, all students would benefit.

"Schools should maintain well-stocked and managed libraries" (p. 119).

It was not the purpose of the report to suggest where the resources to carry out this recommendation should come from, but generally speaking, well-stocked and well-managed libraries tend to show up in school districts that are relatively wealthy. Such school districts are not usually the ones with large numbers of minority students, so the resource issue becomes paramount. However, if this recommendation alone were taken to heart by the nation, and if the schools were set up to allow children maximum use of those libraries, we could see a dramatic increase in the reading, and most likely the reading ability, of minority children. Unfortunately, the current sociopolitical climate is such that we are more likely to continue to have library budgets cut than increased.

"Parents should read to preschool children and informally teach them about reading and writing," and "Parents should support school-aged children's continued growth as readers" (p. 117).

One cannot quarrel with these recommendations themselves. The lives of schoolteachers would be much easier if all children came to school having been read to from a very early age, having a library card and their own library of books, and having had their progress monitored by their parents, their TV viewing guided and limited, etc. The problem with *BNR* is that it doesn't deal adequately with the reality that for some minority parents it is simply not possible to follow these recommendations. The report skirts the issue of how best to deal with children whose parents cannot buy books and are so exhausted from simply trying to support themselves and their families that they must depend totally on the school to make their children readers. Nor does *BNR* address the problems of minority parents who for one reason or another, such as poor educational experiences or a first language other than English, are not comfortable enough with their own reading of English to read to their children or help with homework. In addition, the report offers few, if any, recommendations that would truly capitalize on the language strengths that many minority children bring to school. More important, the report tends to downplay any such strengths, seeing some children, for example, "jump[ing] to incorrect conclusions" (p. 32), whereas researchers who have actually worked with children view the same behaviors as strategies for becoming literate (Harste, Burke, and Woodward 1984).

"Preschool and kindergarten reading readiness programs should focus on reading, writing, and oral language" (p. 117).

In its recommendation to the parents of preschoolers, *BNR* recognizes the factors that have traditionally been correlated with success in school reading programs. However, its recommendations about preschool and kindergarten reading readiness programs may not be as useful for the children who have traditionally not been successful — too frequently, minority children. I certainly have no quarrel with the recommendation that preschool and kindergarten programs focus on reading, writing, and oral language. However, in the discussion of reading, there is too much emphasis on reading *instruction* and not enough on the importance of reading and being read to. Particularly for minority children who have not had the typical white middle-class or upper middle-class home experience that fits so easily with school expectations, kindergarten becomes the place where they need to acquire new experiences with written stories, books, and poems — that is, written language in its many varieties. These children need opportunities to become acquainted with the cadences and conventions of written language *before* they start working formally with the bits and pieces that make up that written language. They need a sense of what literacy has to offer beyond what they already know.

"Reading primers should . . . give children opportunities to apply phonics" (p. 118).

The problem here is that reading materials written to provide practice on phonics are contrived — at best. Minority children need for their initial reading experiences, as do all children, materials that are meaningful and that reflect natural language patterns. This is particularly true for children who have not had much experience with book literacy. The danger is that the emphasis on phonics-driven reading materials, even at the beginning — perhaps *especially* at the beginning — may give children a sense that learning to read is not worth the effort: what they are expected to read has no value to them; it offers none of the richness of real, natural language.

"Children should spend more time in independent reading" (p. 119).

Again, I can only support this recommendation, and perhaps suggest that it might go even further. The potential problem lies in the following statement earlier in the report: "For each age, there are fables, fairy tales, folk tales, classic and modern works of fiction and nonfiction that embody the core of our cultural heritage. A person of that age cannot be considered literate until he or she has read, understood, and appreciated these works" (p. 61). The only examples mentioned of this core literature are "Goldilocks and the Three Bears" and *Peter Rabbit*, both prescribed for kindergartners. I have no objections to either of those stories; I, too, would expect to find them in many kindergartens. But would the Ananse stories from Africa, or the Juan Bobo stories from Puerto Rico, or Mildred Taylor's *Roll of Thunder, Hear My Cry* find their way onto the list? My concern is how "cultural heritage" is to be defined and who is to determine what literature embodies the core of this heritage. The danger is that the cultural heritage is likely to be defined from a very Eurocentric perspective, and minority children will not find their lives and experiences reflected in the literature they read in school. They may therefore continue to receive the message that they and others like them don't matter. And when that impression is also received by children from the privileged majority, the damage is doubly done.

Conclusion

In relation to minorities and literature, *Becoming a Nation of Readers* is mostly silent, and that may be its biggest problem. Literacy and its benefits are not evenly distributed among the many groups that make up our society. For example, many students in the cultural majority who learn how to read but do not become readers may become quite successful adults. The reason is that the doors of opportunity are open to them by virtue of their membership in a social group that is "more equal" than some others. The real challenge for our schools is to extend literacy and its benefits to those who must fight against great odds to achieve any degree of success. In many cases, those students are members of minority groups. The report offers some suggestions that, if followed, could improve the reading instruction such students receive. In terms of literature, however, the question remains: even if children improve their reading proficiency, what will they read?

References

Harste, J., C. Burke, and V. Woodward. 1984. *Language Stories and Literacy Lessons.* Portsmouth, N.H.: Heinemann.

Rosenblatt, L. 1978. *The Reader, the Text, the Poem: The Transactional Theory of the Literary Work.* Carbondale, Ill.: Southern Illinois University Press.

8 Extending Literacy: Expanding the Perspective

Harold L. Herber
Syracuse University

Joan Nelson-Herber
State University of New York at Binghamton

The chapter "Extending Literacy" in *Becoming a Nation of Readers* is as remarkable for what is not addressed as for what is addressed. Let us consider the latter first.

The authors of "Extending Literacy" discuss three factors that they feel are essential in influencing the extension of students' literacy: the quality of school textbooks, the nature of the instruction that teachers provide, and the opportunities for meaningful practice. Textbooks serve as vehicles through which students gain access to information and ideas related to the various disciplines they study. Texts also serve as vehicles for teaching students the processes by which they derive information and ideas from print. Accordingly, the authors of "Extending Literacy" argue that texts must be well organized and at a level of difficulty appropriate to the subject matter being studied and the level of achievement of students for whom the text is designed. They acknowledge that there is more to text difficulty than factors measured by most readability formulas, and they enumerate these additional factors. They call for texts that reveal not only the substance of a discipline but also the manner in which that discipline is organized and structured.

While asserting that well-written texts are necessary for extending literacy, the authors recognize that such texts are not sufficient for attaining such a goal. They state that "teachers must instruct students in strategies for extracting and organizing critical information from text" (p. 71), and they recommend the explaining, modeling, and monitoring that is characteristic of direct instruction as the way to teach these strategies.

Finally, the authors of "Extending Literacy" discuss two kinds of practice that influence the extension of literacy: practice on specific skills and concepts provided by workbooks and skill sheets, and practice on the whole act of reading provided by silent reading and by "opportunities for speaking, listening, and, particularly, writing" (p. 74). They recognize the potential value in the first type of practice; however, they also acknowledge that the quality of typical workbook and skill-sheet activities is such that these activities generally contribute little to raising the level of students' reading performance. The authors strongly endorse practice in the whole act of reading through extended experiences in independent reading. They note the contributions that such practice makes to vocabulary growth, to gains in reading achievement, and to reading fluency. Similarly, they note the strong contribution to reading performance that comes from practice in writing.

Anyone who thinks seriously about extending literacy will agree with the authors in their estimate of the importance of quality of textbooks, teaching, and practice to attaining that objective. Even while acknowledging the value of what the authors have said, however, one cannot help but be disappointed both in what they failed to address and in what they failed to recommend. In the following sections, we discuss the limitations of the perspective of *Becoming a Nation of Readers* and provide a broader view of literary extension.

Limitations of Perspective

It is ironic that a chapter on extending literacy presents such a limited perspective on the topic. This limited perspective is revealed when the chapter is examined in light of four important questions:

1. Who needs help in extending their literacy skills?
2. What should the instructional context be for providing the help?
3. Who should provide the help?
4. What has been accomplished in efforts to extend literacy?

Who needs the help?

The authors of "Extending Literacy" restrict their discussion principally to the elementary grades. The highest grade level referred to in the chapter is grade 8, and most of the references relate to elementary materials and practices. This restriction is signaled in the introduction to the chapter:

> This chapter deals with three essential factors that influence whether the *young readers* [our emphasis] will be able to extend their skill to meet the challenges of subject matter learning. (p. 61)

Given the nature of literacy needs at secondary and post-secondary levels (Kirsch and Jungeblut 1986), this restriction constitutes a serious limitation to a discussion of the concept of extending literacy.

Implicit in the notion of extending literacy is the belief that the act of reading involves more than the application of basic decoding and comprehension skills. Extending literacy involves what are commonly referred to as higher-order skills, by which readers critically and creatively respond to resources and apply to new situations the ideas they acquire through their reading. In an NAEP study, Kirsch and Jungeblut (1986) indicated that individuals between the ages of twenty-two and twenty-five manifest precisely this need. In discussing the findings from this study, Ronald Mitchell, executive director of the International Reading Association, said,

> The data give us reason to celebrate the fact that nearly all young adults are acquiring basic literacy skills. . . . On the other hand, we are concerned by the fact that, as the report notes, a significant number of individuals are failing to develop advanced reading abilities that will enable them to achieve their full potential in a technologically advanced society. ("Young Adults," 1986, p. 1)

With earlier NAEP studies reporting similar findings for seventeen-year-olds (NAEP 1981), the need for an emphasis on extending literacy beyond elementary levels has been clear for some time. All students at all grade levels, even college-level adults, benefit from instruction that develops, refines, and extends their reading skills. Restricting the focus of discussions and recommendations for such instruction to elementary grades leads to the easily drawn, but mistaken, inference that comprehensive reading programs in elementary grades can equip readers with skills that are sufficient for a lifetime of reading.

What should the instructional context be?

In reading the stated purpose for the "Extending Literacy" chapter, it is reasonable to infer the intention to recommend a broad instructional context for extending literacy:

> This chapter deals with three essential factors that influence
> whether the young readers will be able to extend their skill *to
> meet the challenges of subject matter learning* [emphasis ours]. (p.
> 61)

To those whose orientation toward reading instruction involves them
in the "challenges of subject matter learning," this statement raised
a hope that the concept of extending literacy would be linked with
the concept of developing reading skills while studying course content,
and that the implementation of such instructional programs would
be recommended. In fact, the reference to reading instruction in
subject areas is essentially one of dismissal:

> The idea that reading instruction and subject matter instruction
> should be integrated is an old one in education, but there is
> little indication that such integration occurs often in practice.
> (p. 73)

As a consequence, the authors draw most of their examples of what
they consider to be appropriate instruction from reading lessons in
elementary grades and thus limit their recommendations to this
narrow instructional context.

The dismissal of instruction that integrates the study of reading
with the study of course content on the grounds that it rarely occurs
in practice is inconsistent with the recommendation for "direct
comprehension instruction" even though such instruction "is rare
any place in the curriculum in ordinary classrooms" (p. 73). If
comprehension instruction can be recommended for elementary
reading classes though it rarely occurs, why dismiss recommending
such instruction in content-area classes though it rarely occurs? By
limiting their recommendations in this manner, the authors miss an
opportunity to support efforts to extend students' literacy skills in
instructional contexts beyond elementary-level reading classes.

The research drawn on to buttress the recommendations similarly
limits the instructional context for extending literacy. The authors
recognize research that was conducted, in the main, in elementary
reading classes. In so doing, they reinforce the traditional belief that
reading should be taught in reading classes but not in content-area
classes. Further, when they discuss the values of direct instruction
within the context of "reading lessons" in elementary-level reading
classes, they perpetuate the dichotomy between teaching reading and
teaching course content. They give little support or encouragement
to instructional efforts that extend literacy through content-area
studies at secondary and college levels. Limited but highly publicized
recommendations of this sort can lead to actions by influential but

less well-informed individuals that result in the inappropriate imposition of some elementary-level practices on secondary-level instruction; for example, the recent call by the secretary of education for secondary-level projects for the National Diffusion Network "that use such phonics methods to teach reading" ("Notice Inviting," 1986).

Who should provide the help?

With the perspective on the need for extending literacy limited principally to elementary-level students, and with the instructional context for a response to the need limited principally to reading lessons in elementary-level classes, it is easy to infer the authors' opinion on who should provide the instruction: elementary-level teachers. It is reasonable to believe that elementary teachers should bear some responsibility for extending students' literacy. They are already responsible for teaching all subjects, including reading, and they are in a position to help students extend their literacy skills in and through all of their subjects, if they so choose. Even so, the responsibility should not fall *exclusively* on elementary teachers.

The message of "Extending Literacy" leaves unchallenged the multiplied thousands of subject-area teachers in secondary schools whose students are in need of instruction that extends literacy skills beyond basic word recognition and basic comprehension. As is true of their elementary-school colleagues, secondary-school teachers are in a position to help students extend their literacy skills in and through all of their subjects, if they so choose. Given the comprehensiveness of the need for extending literacy, it is appropriate to recommend the most comprehensive response to the need; that is, *all* teachers at *all* grades in *all* subjects should be involved in extending their students' literacy skills. When challenged and when shown how to respond to the challenge, secondary-school teachers can do much to extend their students' literacy skills in and through the study of subject matter.

What has been accomplished?

Either by design or default, the authors of *BNR* severely limit the research and practice they recognize as being related to the idea of extending literacy. This limitation is manifested in two ways: (1) the narrow interpretation of the research and practice cited, and (2) the wide array of research and practice *not* cited.

The research cited to support the recommendations for good texts, good teaching, and good practice is given a narrow interpretation. As already noted, this interpretation led to the virtual exclusion of a consideration of content-area classes in secondary schools as an appropriate instructional context for efforts to extend students' literacy skills. A contrasting interpretation is that research that supports good instructional practice at the elementary level and in reading classes also supports good instructional practice at the secondary level and in content-area classes. It is as appropriate and necessary to have *good texts, good teaching,* and *good practice* in content-area classes as it is to have them in reading classes, and to have them in secondary schools as well as to have them in elementary schools. The same can be said for other dimensions of instruction: activating students' prior knowledge for anticipation and prediction of ideas in text, developing students' technical vocabulary, guiding students' metacognitive abilities related to comprehension, supporting students' independent application of skills and ideas, etc. Because the authors limited their recognition of what is possible at all grade levels in the development of instructional programs for extending literacy, they necessarily limited their recommendations of what should be done. Expanding the perspective on the applicability of research to instruction in content areas and in secondary schools, however, leads to an expansion of the opportunities to extend students' literacy throughout their entire educational experience.

Acknowledging the array of available references to research and practice related to extending literacy reveals much more support for "the idea that reading instruction and subject matter instruction should be integrated" than is recognized in "Extending Literacy." The comprehensive history of content-area reading includes reports on such research and program development over several decades (Moore, Readence, and Rickelman 1983). Sections in *The Handbook of Reading Research* (Pearson 1984) report on a variety of instructional strategies that are useful in extending literacy in and through content areas in secondary schools. Such instructional programs were supported and reported by NDEA and Project English in the 1960s and 1970s, by Cooperative Research projects in the 1960s and 1970s, by Right to Read and Basic Skills programs in the 1970s and 1980s, and by dozens of doctoral dissertations. An examination of such research and program development conducted over the past few decades reveals strategies and practices that can be effectively applied by content-area teachers in their attempts to extend literacy by integrating instruction in reading with instruction in course content. Explications of these strategies and practices can be found in more than twenty professional texts that deal with the topic of integrating the teaching of reading and writing with the teaching of course content (e.g., Dishner et al. 1986; Herber 1978; Moore et al. 1986; Vacca and Vacca 1986). Comprehensive programs exist in a variety of school districts across the country (Herber and Nelson-Herber 1984), and directors of such programs can be found among the memberships of special-interest groups for secondary reading in IRA and AERA as well as among the memberships of NRC, NCRE, and NCTE.

Extending Literacy: A Broader View

Data from NAEP and experience in schools suggest that the need for extending literacy is broadly based: all students at all grade levels evidence this need, including young adults in college. The context for extending literacy can include both reading classes and content-area classes. Instruction that extends literacy can be provided by both reading teachers and content-area teachers. Reading teachers can help content teachers define reading and writing processes that can be instructionally integrated with course content. Content-area teachers, in turn, can help reading teachers identify and select concepts from their disciplines that can be instructionally integrated with reading and writing processes.

Extending literacy involves instructional activities that prepare students for the study of specific concepts and for the application of specific processes. For example, students can be shown how to use their prior knowledge of a topic to anticipate and predict meaning as they read related texts. They can be taught to monitor their reading for consistency or conflict with their prior knowledge in order to confirm their understandings or to construct new knowledge (Nelson-Herber 1985). Extending literacy involves helping students move beyond the application of word-recognition skills to the development of word-acquisition skills as they encounter technical vocabularies essential to the study of concepts under consideration (Nelson-Herber 1986).

Extending literacy also involves showing students how to read and interpret resources essential to the study of various disciplines. This "showing how" involves guiding students in such a way that they develop a sense of how their minds work as they interpret and apply ideas derived from their reading (Herber 1978, 1984; Thompson and Frager 1984; Dishner et al. 1986; Moore et al. 1986; Vacca and Vacca 1986).

In addition, extending literacy involves helping students develop independence in the application of the skills and concepts they have learned. This independence is developed by showing students how to refine, extend, and share the concepts and processes they acquire as they read and respond to the resources required for the study of various disciplines (Herber and Nelson-Herber 1987).

Basic literacy is the foundation of efforts to extend literacy, a foundation derived from effective beginning reading programs. Well-written texts, effective teaching, and appropriate practice at the elementary level are necessary but not sufficient for extending literacy. The instructional need extends beyond the elementary grades, and the instructional context extends beyond the reading class. There are secondary schools, as well as elementary schools, in which students' literacy is being extended by instruction provided in content areas. While much remains to be done, the promise of such instruction is that it will extend literacy for students at every level of reading proficiency.

References

Dishner, E., T. Bean, J. Readence, and D. Moore. 1986. *Reading in the Content Areas.* Dubuque, Iowa: Kendall/Hunt.

Herber, H. 1978. *Teaching Reading in Content Areas.* 2nd ed. Englewood Cliffs, N.J.: Prentice-Hall.

———. 1984. Subject Matter Texts — Reading to Learn. In *Learning to Read in American Schools,* ed. R. Anderson et al. Hillsdale, N.J.: Erlbaum.

Herber, H., and J. Nelson-Herber. 1984. Planning the Reading Program. In *Becoming Readers in a Complex Society,* ed. O. Niles and A. Purves. Chicago: National Society for the Study of Education.

———. 1987. Developing Independent Learners. *Journal of Reading* 30: 584–88.

Kirsch, I., and A. Jungeblut. 1986. *Literacy: Profiles of America's Young Adults.* Princeton, N.J.: Educational Testing Service.

Moore, D., S. Moore, P. Cunningham, and J. Cunningham. 1986. *Developing Readers and Writers in the Content Areas.* New York: Longman.

Moore, E., J. Readence, and R. Rickelman. 1983. An Historical Exploration of Content Area Reading Instruction. *Reading Research Quarterly* 18: 419–38.

National Assessment of Educational Progress. 1981. *Three National Assessments of Reading: Changes in Performance, 1970–1980.* Reading Report No. 11-R-01. Denver: Education Commission of the States.

Nelson-Herber, J. 1985. Anticipation and Prediction in Reading Comprehension. In *Reading, Thinking, and Concept Development,* ed. T. Harris and E. Cooper. New York: The College Board.

———. 1986. Expanding and Refining Vocabulary in Content Areas. *Journal of Reading* 29: 7.

Notice Inviting Applications for New Developer Demonstrator Awards under the National Diffusion Network Program for Fiscal Year 1987. 1986. *Federal Register* 51:180: 33002, Wed., September 17.

Pearson, P., ed. 1984. *Handbook of Reading Research*. New York: Longman.

Thompson, L., and A. Frager. 1984. Teaching Critical Thinking: Guidelines for Teacher-Designed Content Area Lessons. *Journal of Reading* 28: 122–27.

Vacca, R., and J. Vacca. 1986. *Content Area Reading*. Boston: Little, Brown.

Young Adults Have Basic Skills, According to New NAEP Report. 1986. *Reading Teacher* 4, no. 3 (Dec./Jan.): 1.

9 A Principal's Perspective

Bonnie C. Wilkerson
Wild Rose School
St. Charles, Illinois

I read *Becoming a Nation of Readers* from the perspective of one who has the opportunity on a daily basis to be an observer in a multitude of classrooms and to be privy to the successes and failures, joys and frustrations of teachers as they work to facilitate the development of literacy in children. I have watched children emerge literate, with a love of the written word and proficiency in its use. I have also watched children stumble in the process of becoming literate and engage in a struggle to learn that is overpowering in its effects on the whole child. Further, I have watched an alarming majority of students progress consistently and successfully through a carefully managed reading program and emerge having mastered the requisite skills of literacy but viewing their literacy as a series of school tasks rather than as keys to unlock the world around them.

My reactions to *Becoming a Nation of Readers* are strong: many are positive; as many are negative. While my goals are similar to those expressed in the report, I question the wisdom of the direction in which the report attempts to lead us.

Throughout *BNR*, the discussions of the elements needed in instruction and the areas of teachers' influence seem to lead always to the idea that better textbooks and teachers better trained in the use of textbooks will result in better literacy education. The report, however, ends with a call for the "verified practices" of the "best teachers" in the "best schools" to be introduced throughout the country (p. 120). My reaction to *BNR* begins with a sample of some of the "best" I have observed as an educator and administrator.

Mrs. Y's Classroom: Experience Extended through Literacy

Mrs. Y begins the day in her second-grade classroom with a discussion planned around a topic of immediate relevance to her students; for example, the gerbils' new babies, the upcoming Halloween parade, the changing leaves on the tree outside the window. Students participate in the discussion, observing, analyzing, and sharing. Mrs. Y skillfully brings into the language of the discussion one or more words that may be unfamiliar to the children but which carry much meaning in the topic being discussed. The meaning becomes real to the students in the course of the discussion.

Following the discussion, the children begin to write. They are writing a "good-morning" letter to Mrs. Y. The letter is an extension of the discussion just held. It is the children's opportunity to communicate personally with the teacher, to engage her fully with their thoughts and feelings. Later in the day, Mrs. Y will write a response to each letter. Her responses will be personal, they will include comments directed toward the students' comments, and they will contain specialized vocabulary that the students have "tried out" in their letters, thus reinforcing their vocabulary enrichment. Her responses will also include words that she notes students have struggled to spell, erase, and spell again. In writing her responses Mrs. Y takes cues from her students. Her responses demonstrate a sensitivity to children as well as an awareness of their daily readiness to learn and of the "teachable moment" in each letter. She knows her responses will be carefully read and that her students will be eager to write tomorrow's letter. Her students have learned that the richer their letters, the more interesting her responses will be. Mrs. Y's purpose is the development of literacy. Her students are learning to read and write for purposeful communication. Her teaching is an art.

Literacy development is a primary goal throughout each day in the classroom described above. Mrs. Y reads to the class. Students read books and stories to themselves and to each other. They practice reading favorite stories into tape recorders to perfect their oral presentation, and then entertain the class by reading the stories aloud.

Mrs. Y takes dictation from individual students, from groups, and from the class. The dictations are drawn from the children's experiences, and many times they relate to the content areas being explored in the classroom. "Word banks" are developed from the dictated accounts. The word banks are used by students as Mrs. Y guides them in the development of phonics and word-analysis concepts. They are also used by students as the students investigate word concepts and relationships and as the students manipulate and experiment with the structure of language. Mrs. Y has several sets of basal readers that she uses with some groups of readers as they share the same story, predicting outcomes, interpreting, and developing group comprehension.

In short, Mrs. Y's classroom is a learning laboratory. There are opportunities for students to observe, record, and analyze. The foundation of her teaching is experience extended through oral and written language. Mrs. Y's goals and objectives are clear and are based on her knowledge of the development of each child. She is teaching reading, writing, spelling, math, social studies, and science. However, it is impossible to speak of one subject without another in observing her classroom. Instruction is integrated, relevant, personal, literate, and enthusiastic. Her students learn to read and to write. They also develop an enjoyment of reading and writing and a perspective of their literacy as an important part of who they are and what they do.

Skilled Reading and the Whole Language Approach

The first chapter of *BNR* describes skilled reading as constructive, fluent, strategic, and motivated, as well as a lifelong pursuit. Instruction that emphasizes these qualities is inherent in the classroom described above. The report also calls for the following: reading materials that use familiar words and sentence structure, a balance of oral reading for a purpose and silent reading for a purpose, adequate preparation for reading, meaningful discussion, and well-formed children's stories. These are all integral elements of the classroom described above. In addition, instruction in Mrs. Y's classroom answers *BNR*'s concern for phonics instruction that is relevant to the stories read and to the needs of children. Mrs. Y's instruction also incorporates immediate application of reading instruction to nonfiction texts as well as fiction and meets the challenge of moving children from simple stories into subject-matter text through integration of content-area reading instruction. Other *BNR* concerns that are met through the instruction described above include less seatwork with workbooks and skill sheets, more extended writing, a priority given to independent reading, more "engaged time" in reading, and flexible grouping.

Nonetheless, *BNR* dismisses the type of instruction described above, citing "indifferent" test results for such reading instruction, which it groups under "whole language approaches" (p. 45). *Indifferent* here means that the test results were no better but no worse than with other approaches. The fallacy of this argument in regard to the effectiveness of an approach to reading instruction can be articulated in the very language of the report, which states that current tests "give an impoverished picture of reading competence" (p. 99).

The tests referred to here are product measures. They are limited in what they sample and are bound by the assumptions about reading that they represent. Recent studies, however, bound by the common assumption that meaning is constructed by teachers and students through their interaction with each other and with the objects and materials of instruction, have described qualitative differences in learning in varying instructional frameworks (Davidson 1985, 1986; Padak 1986; Wilkerson 1986). They have demonstrated that the way teachers structure lessons, distribute content, and establish expectations for participation influence what is learned (Green, Harker, and Golden 1987), and they have explored how teachers' and students' perceptions of a curricular task — their assumptions and purposes — influence what and how much they learn (Alvermann 1986). *BNR,* however, leads us not toward a focus on the teacher and learner in instruction but toward the development of better textbooks — toward reliance on books that give "adequate explanations" (p. 71). The report ignores the role of the student as a constructive participant in learning and places the teacher in the role of a giver of information whose task it is to follow the organization of a well-written textbook.

Issues in Curriculum and Staff Development

There is no doubt that in the majority of classrooms in this nation, textbooks are the organizing elements of the curriculum and the driving force in instruction. Why this adherence to textbooks as curriculum? The administrative answer to this question in regard to reading instruction is quite clear: the basal reader is used to provide continuity and quality control in instruction. What I fear and what I see as a public school administrator is adherence to a safe middle ground, with teaching viewed as management of instruction. However, continuity and quality control through textbooks, and accountability based on tests that have been denounced as inadequate, do not help us accomplish our goal of excellence in literacy education. Stauffer has warned that

> we must give attention to the most effective ways of challenging the thinking of children, capitalize on their curiosity and individual differences, encourage intellectual explorations, and above all avoid ritualizing instruction through memorization and rote learning. (1980, p. 18)

Literacy requires the use of language as an implement of thought. Language used to examine or convey experience and action develops a correspondence between language and experience that is "most strikingly involved in reading and writing, in school learning, and in other abstract pursuits" (Bruner, Oliver, and Greenfield 1966, p. 322). And yet we find literacy education ritualized through the use of published materials that exist apart from the experiences and actions of students. Nearly twenty years ago Philip Coombs said,

> Nobel prizes are won in science for challenging and upsetting old truths and discovering new ones. The same wholesome irreverence for the "time honored truths" must somehow be instilled into the enterprise that is supposed to breed Nobel prize winners. (1968, p. 167)

Yet we find a majority of schools, now supported by information in *BNR*, depending on textbooks to bring information to students rather than involving students in active learning through examined experience.

Continuity in Instruction

Continuity in an instructional program is an important element, deserving focused attention. This element should be provided through a written curriculum based on a stated philosophy and including goals for instruction. A basal series is a poor substitute for a curriculum, though it may be one tool in implementing the curriculum. School administrators have an obligation to facilitate the development of written curricula based on a foundation of knowledge of child development, learning, and the learning process. Through a written curriculum, the continuity of instruction may be based on achievement of broader goals, with flexibility in learning experiences and materials personalized to the needs and experiences of students. Relying on a set of commercially published materials to organize instruction does disservice to teachers, as it deprives them of the freedom to provide learning experiences they know are valuable for their students. It further does disservice to students, as it deprives them of the best in teaching and learning.

Quality Control in Instruction

Maintaining quality control through standard materials is likewise misdirected. The logic of such "quality control" is that although teachers vary in their abilities, consistent use of the same materials will ensure that all students are exposed to the same instruction, at least in content. Yet, as *BNR* notes, "there are no 'teacher-proof' materials" (p. 85). For the sake of ensuring a structure for less competent teachers, a structure is mandated for all, thus handicapping competent teachers as they find little or no time to provide the learning experiences they perceive as effective means toward growth in literacy. Teachers are told implicitly and explicitly that the road to good teaching is following the right manual.

Quality control is a direct concern and responsibility of the instructional leader, the principal. *BNR* notes that "instructional leadership in reading entails a considerable amount of specialized knowledge and experience" (p. 112). I wholeheartedly agree. Principals have an obligation to be informed and knowledgeable in the same areas expected of teachers. One primary role is to provide supervision directed at ensuring the quality of teaching. Principals also have a primary responsibility to staff their classrooms with competent teachers and rid their classrooms of teachers who remain less than competent. They must be sensitive observers who are able to perceive the value of the instructional activities taking place in classrooms and able to make qualitative judgments about teaching/learning, going beyond the quantitative measures used so extensively to evaluate the effectiveness of instruction.

The need for ongoing and relevant staff development for teachers and administrators is a crucial one. Development of a shared commitment to a philosophy of instruction and implementation of instruction consistent with that philosophy require knowledge, experience, and support. As noted in *BNR,* teachers' knowledge can best be extended through staff development over time with consultant support through classroom visits and through the shared experiences and support of colleagues. However, gaining experience requires the freedom to attempt changes in an environment in which such risk taking is supported by principals and supervisors who understand the value of the changes being attempted. These are concerns for those responsible for teacher and administrator inservice education as well as for institutions that train and certify principals.

Conclusion

I agree with the need to incorporate into curricula many of the elements in reading instruction noted by the authors of *BNR.* Those elements are noted in the earlier analysis of the sample second-grade classroom. However, I disagree with *BNR*'s apparent advocacy of dependency on textbooks to guide instruction. I believe the keys to superior education are people issues: teachers who are more than managers, who are knowledgeable and artful facilitators of student learning; and supervisors who are knowledgeable and artful facilitators of teaching and evaluators of teaching effectiveness. The responsibility for improvement in literacy education does not lie in textbooks. That responsibility is in the hands of administrators as they help to build foundations from which teachers may work and as they support the day-to-day efforts of teachers. Responsibility also lies in the hands of teachers as they guide students in the development of their literacy. Administrators and teachers must work together toward a vision that includes an understanding of what the goals are in literacy education and how students may best be guided on the journey to attainment of those goals.

References

Alvermann, D. 1986. Discussion: The Forgotten Language Art. Paper presented as part of the symposium "Exploration of the Reading Curriculum of Secondary School Content Area Classrooms" at the annual meeting of the American Educational Research Association, San Francisco.

Anderson, R., E. Hiebert, J. Scott, and I. Wilkinson. 1985. *Becoming a Nation of Readers: The Report of the Commission on Reading.* Washington, D.C.: National Institute of Education.

Bruner, J., R. Oliver, and P. Greenfield. 1966. *Studies in Cognitive Growth.* New York: Wiley.

Coombs, P. 1968. *The World Educational Crisis: A Systems Analysis.* New York: Oxford University Press.

Davidson, J. 1985. What You Think Is Going On, Isn't: Eighth Grade Students' Introspections of Discussions in Science and Social Studies Lessons. In *Issues in Literacy: A Research Perspective* (34th NRC Yearbook), ed. J. Niles and R. Lalik. Rochester, N.Y.: National Reading Conference.

———. 1986. The Teacher-Student Generated Lesson: A Model for Reading Instruction. *Theory into Practice* 25: 84–90.

Green, J., J. Harker, and J. Golden. 1987. Lesson Construction: Differing Views. In *Schooling in Social Contexts: Qualitative Studies,* ed. G. Noblit and W. Pink. Norwood, N.J.: Ablex.

Padak, N. 1986. Teachers' Verbal Behaviors: A Window to the Teaching Process. In *Solving Problems in Literacy: Learners, Teachers, and Researchers* (35th NRC Yearbook), ed. J. Niles and R. Lalik. Rochester, N.Y.: National Reading Conference.

Stauffer, R. 1980. *The Language-Experience Approach to the Teaching of Reading.* 2nd ed. New York: Harper and Row.

Wilkerson, B. 1986. Inferences: A Window to Comprehension. In *Solving Problems in Literacy: Learners, Teachers, and Researchers* (35th NRC Yearbook), ed. J. Niles and R. Lalik. Rochester, N.Y.: National Reading Conference.

10 Positive and Negative Choices: Impact on Curricula

Gay Su Pinnell
The Ohio State University

Becoming a Nation of Readers provides a succinct and readable condensation of the collective thinking of many reading researchers and educators. The National Academy of Education's Commission on Education and Public Policy, under whose auspices *BNR* was produced, was established "to bring . . . cross-disciplinary knowledge of research in education to bear in identifying bodies of research that might inform educational policy" (pp. vii–viii). Since Anderson et al. examined the large body of literature generated by researchers in a field that is divided, the inevitable result was a compromise document. While this synthesis brings the field together, it also makes it difficult for the authors because every group can find some fault with the ideas presented.

In this paper I am proposing that the key to the impact of *BNR* lies *outside* the document. The critical decisions rest with board members, teachers, and administrators who read the volume and have responsibility for intelligently and sensitively responding to its recommendations. For that reason, we cannot guarantee the outcomes of any set of broad recommendations, even if they are based on research. Each idea is played out in the social and cultural context of the classroom, the school, the school district, or the state educational system. For each, we can predict a range of potential consequences.

A group of researchers and educators from a variety of areas recently analyzed recommendations from all the recent major reports from *A Nation at Risk* (1983) to *A Nation Prepared* (1986) and conducted a survey of school responses to those reports. Based on their own experiences in policy making and on the school survey, they attempted to predict the potential positive and negative outcomes of selected recommendations. Their report (Wayson et al. 1988a) identified nine recommendations from *Becoming a Nation of Readers* and explicated expected gains and enduring concerns for each.

This paper presents further analysis of those extracted recommendations and shows that each has potential for good or poor results. Implemented by thoughtful and knowledgeable educators, each action could have positive outcomes; applied by noncaring, incompetent, or less knowledgeable educators, the action could be dangerous and destructive. Educational practitioners and policymakers control the delicate balance between these gains and concerns. Their assumptions, decisions, interpretations, and actions are the determining factors.

The critical role that school personnel play in educational reform has recently been given attention by prominent bodies such as the Carnegie Commission (1986) and The Holmes Group (1986). The ability to make thoughtful, knowledgeable decisions seems to be important not only for those we generally call policymakers but for those who put policy into practice — teachers and building principals. It is especially important for those who are responsible for teaching reading. The daily decision making about the reading curriculum determines whether youngsters effectively learn to read and write. Local educators create reading curricula not just in the designated course of study but in what they do every day — in fact, every minute — in buildings and classrooms, and this "operational curriculum" affects individual children much more than the official curriculum (see Wayson et al. 1988b, chapter 2).

In short, local building personnel* determine whether the outcomes of each recommendation are positive or negative. Teachers can use the recommendations in *BNR* as springboards for creating programs consistent with the way children learn. Or they can use the recommendations to perpetuate or intensify rigid and nonproductive "activities." The latter situation is certainly not what the creators of *BNR* intended. Achieving the former goal will require thoughtful analysis and a good deal of common sense.

The following sections deal with the nine *BNR* recommendations extracted by Wayson et al. 1988a. The recommendations are numbered for reference within this paper. Each is followed by a list of possible gains and enduring concerns.

Recommendation 1: "Preschool and kindergarten reading readiness programs should focus on reading, writing, and oral language" (p. 117).

Expected Gains

Can enrich the curriculum in the early grades.

---

* Hereafter, all school building staff, including the principal, counselors, special reading teachers, and classroom teachers will be called teachers.

Can lead to fewer workbook "exercises" that have little value for developing literacy.

Prevents wasting children's and teachers' time on meaningless activities.

Can stimulate teachers to seek new ways to help young children enjoy books and stories.

Can lead to earlier development of reading and writing.

Can lead to staff development that encourages teachers to learn more about language and literacy development.

Enduring Concerns

May confine the curriculum to drill and repetition and ignore children's natural way of learning through play.

May be interpreted as requiring more worksheets and practice pages of young children.

Could eliminate creative activities such as art and field trips, which have educational value beyond basic reading and writing.

Risks conceptualizing curriculum in a narrow way, focusing on reading skills to the exclusion of creative-thinking and problem-solving activities.

The best learning environments for young children are those that offer carefully designed firsthand experiences, including some activities that look like play but that involve exploration and problem solving. Good classrooms are rich with a variety of experiences and materials (King 1980; Platt, in press). Research on language development (see Jaggar and Smith-Burke 1985; Pinnell and Haussler, in press) further suggests that children need many opportunities to use language for a variety of purposes. They need stimulation and opportunity to learn new skills and discover new ideas (Vygotsky 1978). These findings indicate that the kindergarten and first-grade curriculum should be a broad one, with many activities that challenge children's thinking. The most worrisome aspect of the above recommendation, therefore, would be a dangerous narrowing of the curriculum. If teachers interpret the "focus on reading and writing" tasks as isolated drill or as moving children through existing materials at earlier and earlier ages, good kindergarten classrooms could be made less effective by adding many abstract and dull tasks that to young children have little relationship to their own lives. Similarly, poor teachers will simply purchase more and more commercial "skills" materials and workbooks, and those activities will crowd out the few play and art activities that still exist.

On the other hand, even kindergartens that do not have formal reading instruction may not offer a rich range of productive activities. Instead, children may spend their time in idle play activities, letter/ sound drill, coloring, or stereotypic "art" assignments that have little to do with becoming literate or with imagination and problem solving. Giving more attention to real reading and writing could improve these "cut and paste" curricula.

Children need the opportunity to become engaged with books and stories, to try out their own writing, and to become familiar with print (Cochran-Smith 1984; Genishi and Dyson 1984), and they have surprising knowledge of literacy even at young ages (Harste, Burke, and Woodward 1984; Dyson 1984; Clay 1975; Ferriero and Teberosky 1982). New Zealand classrooms present children in the entry class (age five) with a variety of activities, including "big books," shared writing, and opportunities to do their own writing. Thoughtful educators interpreting the above recommendation would draw on the work of Clay (1975), Graves (1983; Graves and Hansen 1983), Bissex (1980), DeFord (1984), and others in improving literacy programs in the early grades. Many children today have little opportunity for exposure to literature and reading activities at home; therefore, it is important for opportunities at school to increase. Effective responses to this recommendation can provide more opportunities and greatly enhance the curriculum for young children.

Effective educators will (1) make decisions that place priority on maximum opportunities for thinking and problem solving with regard to literacy as well as other activities; (2) create a curriculum that includes reading, writing, and opportunities to use language for real purposes through play and other concrete exploratory activities; and (3) design literacy activities that have a "bias toward text," (Clay 1986); that is, which create maximum opportunities for reading *real* stories and hearing them read aloud, composing their own stories and reading them, and attempting their own writing.

Recommendation 2: "Teachers of beginning reading should present well-designed phonics instruction. . . ., [which] should be kept simple and [which] should be completed by the end of the second grade" (p. 118).

Expected Gains

May encourage new and better ways of teaching children relationships between letters and sounds.

If well-designed, can help teachers and children understand sound/letter relationships better.

May lead to improvement in teaching phonics.

Enduring Concerns

Could lead to more of the same poorly designed phonics lessons.

Could lead to overuse of phonics to the detriment of other, more effective reading strategies.

May deemphasize meaning in learning to read.

May lead to blind following of commercially prepared materials.

Could involve staffs in meaningless debate over methods and materials.

This recommendation is one of the most troublesome in *Becoming a Nation of Readers* because of the fear that it might lead some teachers to increase drill on phonics and neglect other aspects of reading, such as comprehension. Or, it might lead school districts to purchase more phonics materials in addition to those already in use. Drill on isolated letters and sounds and "independent" work on worksheets can consume a great deal of reading instruction time. Visual features of print and letter-sound relationships represent valuable information that young readers must learn to use, but they must focus primary attention on meaning; otherwise, reading will become an abstract and mechanical task. From the beginning, children must learn to "orchestrate" a range of strategies for constructing meaning from written texts (Bussis et al. 1985; Clay 1986). Phonics represents only one source of information; others include the readers' life experiences, knowledge of syntactic patterns, and meaning. The most powerful sources, according to Clay (1986), are meaning and language structure. For a reader to become independent, use of visual information must be integrated with those systems.

Some researchers have warned against the overuse of phonics (Goodman 1967, 1970; Smith 1971). Since phonics dominates reading instruction today and many children are still having difficulty in reading, we need to ask ourselves the following: how much phonics instruction is necessary? What kind of phonics instruction is best? Do we need some new and more integrated ways of teaching relationships between letters and sounds? *BNR* seems to be calling for new and better ways of helping children learn phonics, with the ultimate goal of helping them read written language. The key may be in new approaches that link reading and writing (see Mason, in press) and that give children opportunities to analyze words as they construct them in writing stories and messages for their own purposes. As noted in *BNR*, "Opportunities to write have been found to contribute to knowledge of how written and oral language are related, and to growth in phonics, spelling, vocabulary development, and reading comprehension" (p. 79).

Regarding Recommendation 2, effective educators will (1) find opportunities for children to construct their own knowledge of phonics as they engage in reading and writing, (2) ensure that the major part of reading instruction is spent on actual reading of stories and other interesting material, (3) explore new ways to promote children's writing in the early years of school, (4) conduct information sessions to examine research on phonics, and (5) avoid overuse of commercial materials and, instead, work to understand the processes involved in learning to read.

Recommendation 3: "Teachers should devote more time to comprehension instruction" (p. 118).

Expected Gains

May increase teachers' awareness of strategies related to comprehension.

Helps teachers and consequently children to focus on the real purpose of reading — to construct meaning from text.

May require teachers to focus on higher-level strategies rather than memorization or mechanical tasks.

Promotes reading as a whole process.

Enduring Concerns

Could lead to superficial attempts to directly teach comprehension, which is a complex cognitive process.

Requires greater knowledge of comprehension on the part of teachers, textbook writers, and reading experts.

May lead to exercises called comprehension practice but which do not really help readers become better at comprehending text.

Comprehension is always designated as the primary goal of reading, but in general, teachers are insecure about teaching reading comprehension and about measuring it. There are complex issues (see Johnston 1983) related to reading comprehension; for example, is it a process or a product? Can it be measured? Comprehension is an "in the head" process by which the reader links knowledge and experience with the text to construct meaning. Comprehension cannot be directly observed, but it can be inferred from evidence gained through observation of the reader's behavior during reading and while discussing the material read.

Since practitioners find comprehension difficult to understand, they tend to use suggested exercises or questions intended to "check" comprehension. Some even believe that such exercises "teach" comprehension. Recommendation 3 could have positive impact if it results in more emphasis on meaning in reading instruction. On the other hand, the recommendation could lead to expending more time and resources on "comprehension" materials without a thoughtful and critical examination of those materials and the way they are used.

In response to Recommendation 3, effective teachers will (1) learn more about theories of comprehension, (2) learn how to evaluate practices and material that purport to teach comprehension, (3) place priority on time for reading whole stories and books, (4) select reading materials that provide good stories or interesting information, and (5) teach comprehension through doing it — reading, understanding, and talking with others about what was read.

Recommendation 4: "Children should spend less time completing workbooks and skill sheets" (p. 119).

Expected Gains

Frees time that can be spent on actual reading and writing.

Can lead to higher levels of reading during reading instruction.

Prevents wasting time on busywork activities that are not related to reading achievement.

Reduces the cost of materials for teaching reading.

Reduces the frustration some children have with the abstract and sometimes boring tasks required by worksheets.

Decreases the paper load for teachers.

Prevents children's equating reading and writing with filling in blanks.

Enduring Concerns

Poses a problem for teachers' keeping children quiet and busy.

Requires teachers to think of alternatives to workbooks and skill sheets — something they are ill-trained to do.

Makes it necessary to find some new ways of assessing children's work.

Poses a need for staff development to help teachers develop new ways of managing instruction.

Reduces practice of low-level "test taking" skills, which could result in lower test scores.

A salient point in *Becoming a Nation of Readers* is that "the amount of time devoted to worksheets is unrelated to year-to-year gains in reading proficiency (pp. 75–76). A positive response to Recommendation 4 would mean that teachers and children would spend the maximum reading instruction time on actual reading of texts. As Smith (1971) says, we learn to read only by reading; and as mentioned in *BNR*, worksheets provide only a very low level of perfunctory reading. If these two assumptions are true, decreasing time on worksheets and increasing time on reading texts will be of benefit to students.

Implementation of this recommendation, however, may cause management problems for the teacher. The real value of worksheets appears to be that children can work on them independently while teachers work with groups and individuals. Teachers must, then, find other ways for children to work independently. This requirement poses a problem because dependence on materials has been so great for the last twenty years that few teachers know how to manage without them. Staff development and group problem solving will be needed to help teachers take on the new goals. Administrators and policymakers cannot assume that declaring this recommendation to be policy will make it happen.

Regarding Recommendation 4, thoughtful teachers will (1) spend more time on independent writing activities, (2) spend more time on reading texts and less time on filling in workbooks and dittoed materials, (3) work together to design independent activities that will be creative and productive, and (4) work together to solve management problems so that teachers will not become discouraged and fall back into use of dittoed materials.

Recommendation 5: "Children should spend more time in independent reading" (p. 119).

Expected Gains

Provides practice in the whole act of reading rather than on isolated tasks.

Requires school districts and teachers to provide more books and place priority on reading.

Communicates to children the importance of reading.

Can widen children's knowledge in all subject areas.

Provides opportunities for reading that may not be present in children's homes.

Contributes to the improvement of writing.

Helps children connect reading with content/subject matter.

Provides something for children to do instead of seatwork dittoes.

Enduring Concerns

Requires a reallocation of time in the curriculum; some activities must be removed to make way for more reading.

Requires teachers to relinquish some time usually spent on direct instruction.

Requires careful monitoring of students to be sure they are reading.

Requires skill in helping children select appropriate books and talking with them to motivate reading.

May require special skill to help poor readers develop the necessary motivation and ability to read.

Children learn to read by reading; and as they read more, they become better readers. Through reading easy material — sometimes rereading selections many times — children learn to use strategies "on the run" and to increase their fluency and ease in reading (Clay 1986). Those principles suggest that spending more time in independent reading will be of benefit to children. But simply letting children have "free reading" will not guarantee progress, especially for children in the "at risk" groups. Without guidance, follow-up, high expectations, and high-quality interactions with the teacher, time spent on reading may be almost as nonproductive as time spent on dittoed worksheets. For good readers who like reading, the time will be well-used whatever the situation; but in the opposite case, reading time may be wasted rather than used productively. Children often report using Sustained Silent Reading time to daydream, play games, or write notes, especially if the teacher uses the time to grade papers or talk to others. For independent reading to be productive, teachers need to sensitively guide children and provide activities that stimulate interest and allow children to share their reading with others.

In response to Recommendation 5, effective educators will (1) plan for independent reading as a high-priority part of each day, (2) monitor independent reading times to be sure students are reading material they find challenging and interesting, (3) provide instructional activities that are integrated with the independent reading activities and that help in motivating students to read, and (4) work individually with students who find reading difficult to help them use the time productively.

Recommendation 6: "Children should spend more time writing" (p. 119).

Expected Gains

Provides practice in the whole act of writing.

Improves children's performance in all subject areas.

Builds children's ability to sustain a written text.

Helps children make connections between talking, thinking, reading, and writing.

Contributes to the development of reading ability.

Enduring Concerns

Makes it more difficult and time-consuming for teachers to respond to children's writing.

Requires increased knowledge and skill on the part of teachers.

Requires staff development to help teachers understand the writing process.

Requires reallocation of time in the curriculum so that children have appropriate time to write.

Children learn to write by writing. We have learned from recent research (Graves 1983; DeFord 1984) that providing time for writing and paying attention to the process of writing help children become better writers. It is also becoming evident that children can produce written representations of ideas at much earlier ages than has been thought and that there are relationships between the acquisition of writing and the acquisition of reading (Clay 1975; Bissex 1980; Harste, Burke, and Woodward 1985; Goodman and Goodman 1984; Mason, in press). If those assumptions are true, then responding to the recommendation by creating more time for writing should have beneficial effects. As with reading, teachers must approach this recommendation with knowledge and sensitivity, or it can be as destructive and meaningless as the dittoes and worksheets mentioned earlier. Simply assigning and grading writing is not enough. Children who mechanically fill in a journal with the same stereotypical entries every day are not engaged in productive activity. Teachers need to learn more about the processes involved in writing and about how to foster writing in the classroom. Children must write about something, and the environment in the classroom must be structured to elicit purposeful writing that grows out of language and experience (Platt 1984).

In response to Recommendation 6, then, good teachers will (1) allocate sufficient time for in-depth writing experiences, (2) learn more about the processes of writing so that they can more intelligently observe and make decisions about helping children, (3) design classroom experiences so that the experiences lead to writing for a variety of purposes, (4) find ways to help children write for their own purposes, and (5) value children's efforts and find ways to help them share their efforts through class interaction and publication.

Recommendation 7: "Schools should cultivate an ethos that supports reading" (p. 119).

Expected Gains

Indicates a clear sense of purpose among participants in the school.

Requires awareness of environmental factors that support literacy.

Gives attention to the social setting in which reading takes place.

Supports effective classroom instruction.

Has educational benefits beyond reading outcomes.

Enduring Concerns

May require removal of some procedures that are convenient for adults; for example, use of loudspeakers, locked libraries, etc.

If misinterpreted, could create a rigid, nonproductive school climate.

This recommendation recognizes the power of the environment to communicate values and set norms for behavior. School staff can work together on this recommendation to increase morale and a sense of mission in the school (Wayson et al. 1988b). Correctly applied, creating "an ethos that supports reading" could mean a school in which a rich variety of books is readily available to children and the children are given time to read those books. In such a school, children's writing is displayed everywhere in the school, and teachers take time to read books to children and to talk about books. Carried to extremes or rigidly interpreted, however, this recommendation could result in an emphasis on reading instruction to the exclusion of other valuable experiences at school.

In response to Recommendation 7, good educators will (1) work together to design and create a total school atmosphere which communicates that reading and writing are valued, (2) select appropriate literature for classroom libraries in addition to the school library, (3) find opportunities for children to share reading and writing activities outside their own classrooms, (4) involve parents in creating a total environment in which reading and writing are natural and valued activities, (5) place children's reading and writing above adult convenience in the school, and (6) demonstrate an interest in reading themselves.

Recommendation 8: "Schools should maintain well-stocked and managed libraries" (p. 119).

Expected Gains

Provides better access to books.

Stimulates interest in reading.

Communicates the importance of reading.

Offers support to all content areas.

Offers support for writing activities.

Enduring Concerns

Requires trained personnel to make it work successfully.

Requires updated collections of books and other written materials.

Requires cooperation between teachers and library personnel.

May threaten the importance of community libraries.

May reduce teachers' motivation to provide a wide range of literature in the classroom.

The importance of available, well-stocked school libraries seems obvious. Reading materials are often dull and do not provide enough material for avid readers. Many children do not have books in their homes or ready access to public libraries. Libraries are necessary to provide works of literature as well as reference materials for students. Yet libraries are costly and are not as accessible and useful without trained personnel to manage them. Some schools have libraries that are not updated and are often locked because there is no one to supervise their use. In one library, for example, children come once a week to watch a filmstrip because the paraprofessional doesn't know what else to do with the library period. To respond adequately to Recommendation 7, teachers, administrators, and school boards must use creativity to find the necessary resources to provide better libraries in schools.

Recommendation 9: "More comprehensive assessments of reading and writing are needed" (p. 101). (That is, standardized tests should be supplemented.)

Expected Gains

Removes some of the standardized-testing restrictions on curricula.

Provides more meaningful and useful assessments of students' reading and writing.

Educates teachers, administrators, and evaluation personnel on the processes of reading and writing.

Helps teachers in diagnosing students' problems.

Can focus curriculum toward higher-level skills.

Enduring Concerns

Increases time and expense for assessment.

If not implemented properly, could result in more assessment without more learning.

Requires retraining of staff to administer assessments and interpret results.

Requires higher levels of teaching skill.

Recommendation 9 could have negative results if it is interpreted simply to mean more testing; for example, the weekly or daily use of "unit tests" in addition to standardized tests. If, however, "more comprehensive" is interpreted to mean the use of both quantitative and qualitative measures of both children's learning *and* the learning environment, this recommendation could have positive effects. One approach to implementation could be to increase the observational power of teachers and administrators so that they can skillfully and systematically observe and record the reading activity going on in classrooms and in the school as a whole. This observation can provide information that guides teachers in making decisions about individual children and that guides the school staff and principal in making decisions about the curriculum and the school environment.

In response to Recommendation 9, competent educators will (1) gather information about alternative ways of assessing children's learning and reading instruction, (2) expend the time and effort necessary to try out new methods of assessment, (3) use the results of assessment to guide the program, and (4) communicate with parents and others the results of assessment.

Conclusion

Each recommendation by national groups has potential for constructive or destructive results. Even the soundest recommendations and the most effective programs can be misused if teachers or administrators have too little knowledge or skill to implement them. In the hands of competent educators, most of the expected gains will be enhanced and most of the enduring concerns diminished. For that to occur, however, national reports and recommendations must be carefully studied. Educators at all levels must talk about the recommendations with each other and with people who have expertise in the areas concerned. Long-term professional development may be necessary to ensure the competence required to increase the potential for good. School staffs must work together and support each other, especially when taking on approaches that are radically different from those currently in place. Innovations require long-term testing. If we have learned anything in the last twenty years of educational change, it is that there are no "quick fixes."

Whether *Becoming a Nation of Readers* offers positive directions or creates destructive forces is only partially contained in the recommendations themselves. Other factors include our own understanding of children, our understanding of learning, and our understanding of teaching. The list of gains and concerns presented here presumes little change in the professional skills and judgments available in most schools. If gains are to be accomplished, it is necessary to plan for positive implementation of the recommendations.

First Steps

Coping with policy recommendations is always difficult for educators on the firing line. The usual response is for the administrative staff or board to adopt new sets of materials or to call a group together to write new curriculum guides. Sometimes, closer monitoring and supervision systems are installed to ensure that the new practices or materials are used correctly. Those responses seem logical; yet, their results are often mixed. Often, teachers and/or principals do not understand the intent of the innovation, or they adopt the form without the substance of the instructional practice. They either act out the script provided by the central office, or they simply ignore the attempted change and proceed as usual. In fact, the "materials" approach is the most likely to lead to the destructive outcomes I have previously identified for the *BNR* recommendations.

In the first stages of change, "top-down" authority may be — indeed probably is — necessary, but it must be accompanied by understanding among those who must implement it every day. Years of educational reform (Berman and McLaughlin 1975) have shown that innovations which proceed without the responsibility, understanding, and ownership of those involved will ultimately fail. Further, scholars of teacher education and staff development (Carnegie 1986; The Holmes Group 1986) are finally recognizing that teachers, like other professionals, must develop the underlying understandings necessary to make decisions concerning their tasks. In view of the critical nature of teacher understanding, we can suggest only one stance toward *Becoming a Nation of Readers:* teachers and building administrators must thoughtfully and knowledgeably consider the recommendations, decide what those recommendations mean for the education of the children they teach, and frame the recommendations — including acceptance or rejection — in terms of their own environments.

In conclusion, I will propose one process that might be used to make decisions about responses on the local level. This is a flexible process that can be modified according to the needs of those involved. An important point to note is the suggestion that school staffs might want to consult "experts" to develop their own knowledge base for decision making. I strongly suggest that the stance toward these "experts" is a different one from the usual hiring of a consultant to make a speech or "tell us what to do." In the process described below, school staffs first think about the questions they have, then *they* consult the "experts" and make use of the information. This "being in charge" aspect of the process is what creates ownership and serious consideration of theoretical issues involved in decision making. It is also important to note that this process will take several weeks of staff time because it includes staff meetings, individual work, reflection, and group decision making. This development time is an essential part of the decision-making process and cannot be short-circuited.

A Step-by-Step Process for Responding to the Recommendations

1. Have the entire staff read the document carefully.

2. In a staff meeting, generate a list of recommendations from the document. In the first recording, accept every recommendation suggested by participants. Then, as a group, decide whether any can be combined. At this point, do not argue over the recommendations or refuse to accept any that do not seem

to fit the philosophy of the staff. Simply make a concise list, like the one above, that can provide a starting point.

3. Have staff members, in small groups or individually, list "indicators" for each recommendation. Indicators are short statements that describe what a visitor would see happening in the school or classroom if the recommendation were implemented in the school. Ask questions such as the following: "What would we see children doing?" "What would we see teachers doing?" "What materials would we see being used?" The indicators will help staff members understand how they and others can operationalize the recommendation, thus leading to a greater awareness of their own implicit theories.

4. Combine, refine, and discuss the lists of indicators. Identify areas where further information is needed to achieve in-depth understanding of the recommendation.

5. Consult necessary written materials and/or "experts" as necessary to expand the knowledge of the decision makers.

6. Consider the following options:
   A. Select one or two recommendations on which the school staff would like to work together to implement. (An alternative is to have each grade level select one or two recommendations.) Create a plan for following the recommendations as defined in the indicators.
   B. Reject some or all of the recommendations in the document, but create other recommendations.

Whatever the outcomes of the process, the group will have increased their own knowledge and their power as educational decision makers. In this way, whether readers accept or reject the premises of *Becoming a Nation of Readers,* the report will have achieved its basic goal, "to inform educational policy," at the most basic level of the educational system. The document offers the opportunity. What we make of it is our choice and our challenge.

Bibliography

Allington, R. 1977. If They Don't Read Much, How They Ever Gonna Get Good? *Journal of Reading* 21: 57–61.

———. 1980. Poor Readers Don't Get to Read Much in Reading Groups. *Language Arts* 57: 872–76.

Anderson, R., E. Hiebert, J. Scott, and I. Wilkinson. 1985. *Becoming a Nation of Readers: The Report of the Commission on Reading.* Washington, D.C.: National Institute of Education.

Berman, P., and M. W. McLaughlin. 1975. *Federal Programs Supporting Educational Change. Vol. IV: The Findings in Review.* Santa Monica, Calif.: Rand Corporation.

Bissex, G. 1980. *Gnys at Wrk: A Child Learns to Write and Read.* Cambridge, Mass.: Harvard University Press.

Bussis, A., E. Chittenden, M. Amarel, and E. Klausner. 1985. *Inquiry into Meaning: An Investigation of Learning to Read.* Hillsdale, N.J.: Erlbaum.

Carnegie Task Force on Teaching as a Profession. 1986. *A Nation Prepared: Teachers for the 21st Century.* New York: Carnegie Forum on Education and the Economy.

Clay, M. 1975. *What Did I Write?* Auckland, New Zealand: Heinemann.

———. 1979. *Reading: The Patterning of Complex Behavior.* Exeter, N.H.: Heinemann.

———. 1982. *Observing Young Readers.* Auckland, New Zealand: Heinemann.

———. 1986. *The Early Detection of Reading Difficulties.* 2nd ed. Exeter, N.H.: Heinemann.

Cochran-Smith, M. 1984. *The Making of a Reader.* Norwood, N.J.: Ablex.

DeFord, D. E. 1984. Classroom Contexts for Literacy Learning. In *The Contexts of School-Based Literacy,* ed. T. E. Raphael. New York: Random House.

Dyson, A. 1984. Reading, Writing, and Language: Young Children Solving the Written Language Puzzle. In *Composing and Comprehending,* ed. J. M. Jensen. Urbana, Ill.: National Council of Teachers of English and the National Conference on Research in English.

Ferreiro, E., and A. Teberosky. 1982. *Literacy before Schooling.* Exeter, N.H.: Heinemann.

Genishi, C., and A. Dyson. 1984. *Language Assessment in the Early Years.* Norwood, N.J.: Ablex.

Goodman, K. 1982 [1967]. Reading: A Psycholinguistic Guessing Game. In *Language and Literacy: The Selected Writings of Kenneth S. Goodman,* Vol. 1, ed. F. V. Gollasch. Boston: Routledge & Kegan Paul.

———. 1970. Behind the Eye: What Happens in Reading. In *Reading: Process and Program,* ed. K. S. Goodman and O. S. Niles. Urbana, Ill.: National Council of Teachers of English.

Goodman, K., and Y. Goodman. 1984. Reading and Writing Relationships: Pragmatic Functions. In *Composing and Comprehending,* ed. J. M. Jensen. Urbana, Ill.: National Council of Teachers of English and the National Conference on Research in English.

Graves, D. 1983. *Writing: Teachers and Children at Work.* Exeter, N.H.: Heinemann.

Graves, D., and J. Hansen. 1983. The Author's Chair. *Language Arts* 60: 176–83.

Halliday, M. In press. Learning Language, Learning about Language, Learning through Language. In *Negotiating Meaning: Impact of Language*

Research on Schools and Classrooms, ed. G. S. Pinnell and M. Haussler. Urbana, Ill.: National Council of Teachers of English.

Hansen, J. 1984. Learners Work Together. In *The Contexts of School-Based Literacy*, ed. T. E. Raphael. New York: Random House.

Harste, J., C. Burke, and V. Woodward. 1984. *Language Stories and Literacy Lessons*. Portsmouth, N.H.: Heinemann.

Heath, S. 1983. *Ways with Words: Language, Life, and Work in Communities and Classrooms*. Cambridge, Mass.: Harvard University Press.

The Holmes Group. 1986. *Tomorrow's Teachers: A Report of The Holmes Group*. East Lansing, Mich.: The Holmes Group.

Johnston, P. H. 1983. *Reading Comprehension Assessment: A Cognitive Basis*. Newark, Del.: International Reading Association.

———. 1987. Teachers as Evaluation Experts. *The Reading Teacher* (April): 744–48.

King, M. 1980. Learning How to Mean in Written Language. *Theory into Practice* 19: 163–69.

Mason, J. In press. *Reading/Writing Connections: An Instructional Priority in the Elementary School*. Newton, Mass.: Allyn & Bacon.

National Commission on Excellence in Education. 1983. *A Nation at Risk: The Imperative for Educational Reform*. Washington, D.C.: U.S. Government Printing Office.

Platt, N. 1984. How One Classroom Gives Access to Meaning. *Theory into Practice* 239–45.

Shulman, L. S. 1986. Paradigms and Research Programs in the Study of Teaching: A Contemporary Perspective. In *Handbook of Research on Teaching*, ed. M. C. Wittrock. New York: Macmillan.

Smith, F. 1971. *Understanding Reading: A Psycholinguistic Analysis of Reading and Learning to Read*. New York: Holt, Rinehart & Winston.

Taylor, D. 1983. *Family Literacy: Young Children Learning to Read and Write*. Exeter, N.H.: Heinemann.

Tierney, R., and P. Pearson. Toward a Composing Model of Reading. *Language Arts* 60: 568–80.

Wayson, W., et al. 1988a. *Up from Excellence*. Bloomington, Ind.: Phi Delta Kappa.

———. 1988b. *Report of the Phi Delta Kappa Commission on Public Confidence in Education*. Bloomington, Ind.: Phi Delta Kappa.

Vygotsky, L. S. 1977. *Thought and Language*. Cambridge, Mass.: MIT Press.

———. 1978. *Mind in Society: The Development of Higher Psychological Processes*. Cambridge, Mass.: Harvard University Press.

Afterword

The contributors to this volume approach *Becoming a Nation of Readers* from a number of perspectives. Although there are some differences among them, there are also common concerns:

1. *BNR* reflects inconsistent views in its broad description of the reading process and its description of the process of literacy development. The view of the process of reading is cognitive, holistic, and integrative. The view of literacy development vacillates between holistic and atomistic conceptualizations.

2. There is also inconsistency between the view of what constitutes effective reading and the recommendations for instruction to develop effective reading. The recommendations for instruction appear to violate the conditions necessary for effective reading.

3. *BNR* pays too little attention to learners' characteristics and needs. This is particularly true of minority learners.

4. The report also gives too little attention to teachers and shows too little awareness of the strengths and problems of teachers.

Some particular problems are also raised:

1. The research literature is selectively cited. Sometimes this reflects the exclusion of whole bodies of research, such as that supporting whole language. Several critics in this book document the extensive research in whole language and other areas neglected in *BNR*. Sometimes *BNR* appears to represent a highly selective reading of a body of research, such as that on early literacy development. Certain very prominent researchers are missing or hardly noted. In contrast, some not very prominent researchers are heavily represented. This would not be so serious a problem if it were not that the report claims to distill all of the significant research and if this claim were not so widely quoted when the report is cited.

2. Most of the recommendations of the report express laudable sentiments that are neither new nor controversial. Some of these are so broadly stated that they only raise topics without really offering specific directions. For instance, a number of recommendations deal

with parents and reading development. The report says, *Parents should read to their children.* On the face of this who could disagree? But what good does it do to tell illiterate parents to read to their children? What sensitivity is shown to the differences of income, resources, available time, and cultural and linguistic factors? How shall schools approach a full range of parents to help them support literacy in their children?

A few of the recommendations, in contrast, are quite controversial and quite specific. One taken on by several critics in this book is the recommendation on direct instruction of a particular kind of phonics. In the context of the long list of seemingly noncontroversial recommendations, a sense is conveyed that this is an equally uncontested conclusion of the research.

3. There is a strong tendency throughout *BNR* to confuse research on the reading process with research on reading development and research on reading instruction. Therefore, research using various instructional methodologies is used to draw conclusions about how children learn to read. Several of the critics suggest the presence of a bias in *BNR* that equates teaching and learning.

I would like to suggest two underlying reasons for these problems and key weaknesses in the report. First, it is clear that the group who wrote the report was not broad enough. It was a group largely composed of cognitive psychologists who do experimental research. It did not fully represent the research paradigms and disciplines currently at work in the study of literacy: anthropology, linguistics, literary theory, child development, qualitative research, children's literature research, and others. And it did not represent teachers, administrators, and others in the real world of the schools. The narrowness of the team that produced *BNR* explains some of the narrowness of the report and some of its inconsistencies. The report is simultaneously highly sophisticated when it comes to aspects of reading comprehension and incredibly naive when it comes to classroom realities or parent-child interactions, particularly in minority homes.

A second major reason for the flaws in the report is that it has two very different agendas. One agenda is an educational one: to distill from the research on reading what we know will help us become "a nation of readers." The other agenda is a political one. In some of the national reports (for example, *A Nation at Risk*), the political agenda clearly involves an attempt to change the direction of American education. The political agenda of *BNR* is a researcher's political agenda. This agenda operated as a screen or filter on what the report did and didn't include. How would the report hurt or advance the interests of the researchers who produced it? Who are the groups with power who need to be pleased or at least not offended? What are the sensitive areas to avoid? What are the popular areas to stress? How can the report appear to raise critical issues while not offending any power groups? (An example of this is the way the report appears to be critical of basal readers while acknowledging their dominance in the field and in fact supporting continuation of that dominance.)

Becoming a Nation of Readers is remarkably successful as a political document. It won the enthusiastic acceptance of the Far Right. The Reading Reform Foundation, together with *Reader's Digest,* took out a full-page ad in the *New York Times* to proclaim their love for its instructional recommendations, particularly what they call "phonics first." Secretary Bennett and his boss found in it a view of reading they could accept. None of them found anything objectionable in it. The Economy Company, a publisher of phonics-oriented basals, published and distributed free annotated copies showing how their program is consistent with the report. Open Court, another phonics-oriented basal publisher, took out large advertising space in *Education Week* proclaiming that its language arts program was the embodiment of the recommendations in *BNR.*

School authorities have used the recommendations of the report selectively, depending on their purpose, to justify their reading programs. The California Reading Framework, for example, cites it liberally to support their literature-based thrust and to justify de-emphasizing phonics.

And of course the report got generally positive editorials in the newspapers. The report was widely covered in news stories and picked up by several prominent columnists. The recommendations were broadly enough stated that they could appear to journalists to be inclusive and far-reaching.

But no matter how the report succeeded in advancing its political agenda, it failed in its educational agenda. It failed in its own intended purposes. School authorities can use the recommendations selectively to justify what they are already doing (as with the California Reading Framework). But they can't use them, as many have tried, to *build* a reading program or to improve an existing one. There isn't enough substance or consistency for that. Authors and publishers of basals and other instructional materials may take comfort from the report's rhetoric. But they won't find inspiration for new research-based approaches or useful concepts for innovative programs. As the *Report*

Card on Basal Readers (1988) shows, they didn't need *BNR* to tell them to put more phonics in the early grades and less in the later grades. And *BNR* has done nothing to advance knowledge or suggest needed research. The writers opted to claim consensus where none exists. They might have made a greater contribution by stressing the disagreements, the unresolved conflicts, and the unanswered questions. But that might not have gone well with politically powerful groups seeking simple solutions to complex problems.

Could *BNR* have succeeded with both its agendas? Probably not completely. One or the other had to dominate. What dominates *Becoming a Nation of Readers* is its political agenda.

Kenneth S. Goodman
University of Arizona

Reference

Goodman, K., P. Shannon, Y. Freeman, and S. Murphy. 1988. *Report Card on Basal Readers*. New York: R. C. Owen.

Counterpoint and beyond:
The dialogue continues . . .

Jane L. Davidson

Contributors

David Bloome is an associate professor in the reading and writing program in the School of Education, University of Massachusetts at Amherst. He has taught English and reading at the elementary, junior high, and high school levels. He is the editor of *Linguistics and Education: An International Research Journal,* as well as the editor of *Literacy and Schooling* and *Classrooms and Literacy.* Dr. Bloome has published widely on classroom interaction and reading and writing as social processes. He was a member of the NCTE Commission on Reading in 1985–86 and regularly makes presentations at NCTE conferences.

Rudine Sims Bishop is a professor of education at The Ohio State University. She taught elementary school in Pennsylvania for a number of years, and while at Wayne State University was a participant in the Reading Miscue Research Project. For several years, she was on the faculty of the University of Massachusetts, where she directed a graduate-level teacher education program in reading, writing, and literature. Professor Bishop is active in the International Reading Association, and has been elected to several positions in NCTE, for which she is currently a trustee of the Research Foundation. She has been a speaker at numerous national and international conferences, and is the author of several articles and chapters in professional books and journals. She is the author of *Shadow and Substance: Afro-American Experience in Contemporary Children's Fiction.*

Connie A. Bridge is a professor of education in the Department of Curriculum and Instruction at the University of Kentucky, where she teaches courses in reading and language arts. She has taught third grade and special reading classes in elementary schools. Dr. Bridge has published articles and chapters in various professional journals and books and is currently one of the authors of a basal reading series, with primary responsibility for the early levels of the series (K–2). She also makes frequent presentations at reading and language arts conferences and conducts workshops for teachers on reading and language arts.

Cheryl M. Cassidy is a lecturer with the English Composition Board at The University of Michigan. Her recent dissertation on Victorian prose in the periodical press examined the formation of British colonial policy through a new model of cross-textual rhetoric. She has worked as a reading consultant in public schools, has designed and implemented computer writing programs, and is currently working on a book on women's rhetoric in the Victorian period.

Marsha Chapman is a doctoral student in the Department of Curriculum, Teaching, and Psychological Studies at The University of Michigan. She has taught English and reading to students in grades 7–12 and is currently serving as coordinator of The Children's Program at The University of Michigan's Reading and Learning Skills Center. Her research interests are reading cognition and metacognition and classroom teaching processes.

Jane L. Davidson is a professor in the Department of Curriculum and Instruction at Northern Illinois University, where she serves as chair of the Reading Faculty, directs the Reading Clinic, and teaches graduate classes in reading. She has teaching experience at the elementary school level and as a K–12 reading consultant in the public schools. Professor Davidson serves as principal investigator in a line of research focusing on students' processes of comprehension attainment, and has recently coauthored *Directed Reading-Thinking Activities.* She is a regular presenter at local, state, and national reading conferences.

Kenneth S. Goodman is a professor at the University of Arizona. He codirects The Program in Language and Literacy. He is past president of IRA, NCRE, and CELT. Dr. Goodman has done extensive research on the reading process. He won the NCTE David Russell Award for Outstanding Research in English, and has served on the NCTE Commission on Reading and the NCTE Commission on the English Language. In addition, Dr. Goodman coauthored the *Report Card on Basal Readers.*

MaryAnne Hall is a professor of education at Georgia State University, where she teaches undergraduate and graduate courses in children's literature, language arts, and reading. She has written several books and numerous articles. Literacy for beginners and adults is a major interest. Professor Hall has made many presentations at national, state, and local meetings. In addition, she has served as editor of the *Georgia Journal of Reading* and has served on the Publications Committee of the International Reading Association.

Harold L. Herber is a professor of education at Syracuse University, where he is director of the Interdisciplinary Institute on Literacy. He is also codirector of the Network of Demonstration Centers for Teaching Reading in Content Areas. He is author of the professional text *Teaching Reading in Content Areas;* several videotaped staff development programs in reading and writing across the curriculum; and numerous articles and chapters. Dr. Herber has served as director of NCTE's Commission on Reading, as well as a member of the Commission on the English Curriculum. He has also served on IRA's Board of Directors as well as being chair of the Publications Committee and coeditor of the *Journal of Reading.* His interests include the development of advanced literacy skills, content-area reading, staff development, and the instructional use of video.

Joan Nelson-Herber is a professor of education at the State University of New York, Binghamton. She is also codirector of the Network of Demonstration Centers for Teaching Reading in Content Areas, a project originally funded by the U.S. Department of Education in support of staff development, curriculum development, and school-based research in reading comprehension. She is the author of two middle school reading texts, several videotaped staff development programs in reading and writing, and numerous articles in books and professional journals. Dr. Nelson-Herber has served on the NCTE Commission on Reading as well as the IRA committees on Teacher Education and Research and Studies. She has also served as chair of IRA's Publications Committee. Her interests include translating research findings into practical strategies for instruction; staff development; and designing school-based research.

Karla F. C. Holloway is an associate professor of English at North Carolina State University at Raleigh. She is associate editor of *OBSIDIAN II: Black Literature in Review*, and teaches graduate and undergraduate courses in linguistics and black literature. In addition to journal articles that reflect her research in psycholinguistics and child language use and acquisition, Dr. Holloway has authored *The Character of the Word* and coauthored *New Dimensions of Spirituality*. She has made regular presentations at NCTE conventions, is a past member of the NCTE Commission on the English Language, and is a current member of the NCTE Commission on Reading.

Doug Lia is the principal of a K–3 elementary school building and shares curriculum duties for Yorkville Community School District #115 in Yorkville, Illinois. Dr. Lia taught the primary grades for fifteen years before entering the administrative field. He continues to do presentations, workshops, and inservice work in the field of reading.

Gay Su Pinnell is an assistant professor of theory and practice at The Ohio State University. She has taught elementary school and has worked as a consultant for the Ohio Department of Education. In addition to journal articles, book chapters, and presentations to scholarly organizations, she is the editor of and contributor to *Discovering Language with Children* and coauthor of *Teaching Reading Comprehension*. Recently, she provided leadership for the Ohio Reading Recovery Project, a major research and development project sponsored by the Ohio General Assembly. This early-intervention effort focuses on helping failing first graders learn to read. Her current work includes acting as principal investigator for the Early Literacy Research Project, sponsored by the John D. and Catherine T. MacArthur Foundation.

David Schaafsma is a doctoral candidate in English and education at The University of Michigan. A former high school teacher, he is one of the founders of the Huron Shores Summer Writing Institute, a community-based project collaboratively designed by university and high school teachers, students, and community members. He has conducted numerous writing workshops with teachers and students, and has made presentations

112

at NCTE, CCCC, and NCTE affiliate conferences. His dissertation explores the value of narrative in both composition classrooms and research into those classrooms.

Jerrie Cobb Scott is the director of the Center for Studies of Urban Literacy at Central State University, Wilberforce, Ohio. She was formerly the director of freshman English at the University of Florida, where she also taught undergraduate and graduate courses in English and linguistics. Much of her research has focused on language variation, as have her major publications. She coedited *Tapping Potential: English and Language Arts for the Black Learner* and served as editorial consultant for *Studies in Writing and Rhetoric* and *College Composition and Communication*. Dr. Scott regularly conducts workshops in public schools and colleges in the areas of composition, language arts, and language variation.

Cheryl Troyer is an instructor of reading at Northern Illinois University, where she is completing her doctoral studies. She has taught kindergarten, first grade, and special education in Illinois public schools. Ms. Troyer works as a reading/language arts consultant to school districts and parent groups and has made presentations at local, state, and regional conferences. Her major areas of interest include emerging literacy and reading and language use in classrooms.

Bonnie Wilkerson is the principal of Wild Rose Elementary School in St. Charles, Illinois. She holds a doctoral degree in reading from Northern Illinois University. Currently president of the Language Experience Approach Special Interest Council of the Illinois Reading Council, she is also general chair of the Illinois State Young Authors Conference. Formerly a research fellow at Northern Illinois University, she continues to contribute to research on the process of comprehension development. Dr. Wilkerson makes presentations regularly at conferences of the National Reading Conference, the International Reading Association, the American Educational Research Association, and the Illinois Reading Council.